THE LORD NEEDED A PROPHET

SUSAN ARRINGTON MADSEN

SECOND EDITION

Published by
Deseret Book Company
Salt Lake City, Utah

To my parents, Leonard and Grace Arrington, who
taught me in my youth that there is no such word as *can't*

Photographs and illustrations on pages 63, 80, 97 (right), 108, 148, 151, 156, 165,
188, 193, 194, 196, 200, 203, 211, 212, 218, 220, 223, 227, 229, 232, 233, 237,
238, 241, 246, 248, 250, 252, and 255 are from the Visual Resources Library, The
Church of Jesus Christ of Latter-day Saints. The photograph on page 216 is from
the U.S. Department of Agriculture. The illustration on page 12 is from Peck's
Camera Shop. All other photographs and illustrations are from the Church
Archives, The Church of Jesus Christ of Latter-day Saints. Church materials
© by The Church of Jesus Christ of Latter-day Saints. Used by permission.

© 1990, 1996 Susan Arrington Madsen

First edition 1990. Second edition 1996.

Library of Congress Cataloging-in-Publication Data

Madsen, Susan Arrington.
    The Lord needed a prophet / Susan Arrington Madsen. — 2nd ed.
        p.   cm.
    "Cinnamon Tree."
    Includes bibliographical references and index.
    Summary: Examines the lives of the prophets of The Church of Jesus
Christ of Latter-day Saints.
    ISBN 1-57345-088-X
    1. Church of Jesus Christ of Latter-day Saints—Presidents—
Biography—Juvenile literature. 2. Mormon Church—Presidents—
Biography—Juvenile literature. 3. Prophets (Mormon theology)—
Juvenile literature. [1. Church of Jesus Christ of Latter-day
Saints—Presidents. 2. Mormon Church—Presidents.] I. Title.
BX8693.M326   1996
289.3'092'2—dc20   96-31
[B]   CIP
                                                                      AC

Printed in the United States of America   18961-4588B

10   9   8   7   6

Contents

Preface and Acknowledgments

Prophets have special meaning to members of The Church of Jesus Christ of Latter-day Saints. These men are considered to have a holy, important relationship with Heavenly Father. They communicate with him to receive revelations for the Church. The Lord speaks through prophets to inspire, lead, and teach his children on the earth.

In preparing this book, I have realized clearly that the Lord prepared the prophets from their boyhood to be able someday to accept the responsibility of leading the Church. It is exciting to read about how this happened.

As young people, the future prophets played as children played, riding horses, taking piano lessons, and chasing girls at school with caterpillars. They also had deeply spiritual experiences that converted them more fully to the gospel and strengthened their testimonies. They each learned as young men to work hard, thus preparing themselves for the rigorous work they would do for the Lord. There are dramatic stories of the many times Heavenly Father protected them from physical danger, sparing their lives to accomplish a great work. We also read about their families, their missions, their hobbies, and how these experiences shaped their lives.

These men each had different talents, strengths, and personalities that made them unique. Each prophet made different but important contributions to building the kingdom of God on the earth. Studying their lives has been a thrilling experience for me.

Fine biographies have been written of each of the presidents of the Church, and these are helpful to priesthood groups, Relief Societies, and general readers. This book has been written especially for *young people* and their teachers. I have gone to great effort to include true stories and experiences with special meaning for young people. I have talked to descendants of many of the presidents of the Church who have given me permission to use stories that have not gone beyond family conversations until now.

For help in preparing this book, I am grateful to several excellent historians, including my father, Leonard J. Arrington, as well as Ronald W. Walker, Maureen Beecher, Paul T. Smith, Scott Kenney, Glen Stubbs, and John Sant. I appreciate the generous help of Jeff Simmonds and Brad Cole at Utah State University Special Collections.

In the final stretch, I benefited greatly from the wisdom and advice of James Jacobs, children's literature specialist at Brigham Young University. Useful editing suggestions were also made by Leslie K. Austin, Allison G. Dunn, Edward L. Kimball, Helen and Brent Goates, Whit and Alice Smith, Margene Thorpe, and my brothers, James and Carl Arrington.

I express special gratitude to my friend and husband, Dean Madsen, for his full support and constant encouragement. He also read the manuscript and made excellent suggestions. Our four daughters, Emily, Rebecca, Sarah, and Rachel, provided a delightful testing ground for the appropriateness of the vocabulary and stories.

When all is said and done, my greatest hope is that this book will help young Latter-day Saints better understand and love the presidents of the Church.

JOSEPH
SMITH, JR.

BRIGHAM
YOUNG

JOHN
TAYLOR

WILFORD
WOODRUFF

LORENZO
SNOW

JOSEPH F.
SMITH

HEBER J.
GRANT

GEORGE
ALBERT
SMITH

DAVID O.
McKAY

JOSEPH
FIELDING
SMITH

HAROLD B.
LEE

SPENCER W.
KIMBALL

EZRA TAFT
BENSON

HOWARD W.
HUNTER

GORDON B.
HINCKLEY

Joseph Smith, Jr.

A Friend to Everyone

Emma Smith almost dreaded having her husband, Joseph, go outside to work in the family garden. She knew exactly what would happen. No sooner would Joseph begin to weed the first row of carrots than a neighbor would notice him outside and walk over to say hello. Then a few friends passing by the Smith home would hop out of their buggy and join in the conversation. Before long, a whole group of Saints would have surrounded Emma's dear husband, trading stories, asking questions, listening to his wonderful advice and counsel—and trampling Emma's carefully planted garden.

But who could blame them? Certainly Emma didn't. She knew they were hardly thinking of the vegetables growing beneath their feet. Their full attention was focused on Joseph, tall and handsome, leaning against his hoe. The Lord had chosen a friendly, charming, outgoing leader to be the prophet of the Restoration. Joseph loved people, and they loved to be with him. The garden would just have to wait.

The Saints enjoyed hearing Joseph speak—even for hours at a time. They asked him endless questions about the revelations he had received from the Lord. They marveled at his spiritual experiences. Joseph had seen God the Father, the Savior, and other heavenly messengers. His rugged, calloused hands had held the golden plates from which he had translated the Book of Mormon. Joseph was more than the mayor of their bustling community—Nauvoo, Illinois. He was a true prophet of God.

At six feet tall and weighing about two hundred pounds, the Prophet Joseph had an athletic build. He enjoyed hard work and energetic play. Joseph frequently joined the young boys in Nauvoo in outdoor games. He could hit a ball with a bat so great a distance that the other players would call to the boy who was going for the ball to take his dinner while he was at it. Joseph would laugh and go on with the game.

Joseph did everything he could to help the Saints. He gave many of them special blessings to help them with illnesses or problems. He organized log-splitting contests among the men and then gave the wood to families in need. Once, he and some young men were playing ball and began to get tired. He stopped the game, called them together, and said, "Let us build a log cabin." So off they went, Joseph and the young men, to build a log cabin for a widow.

The story of this beloved prophet began in a small cabin in Sharon, Vermont, where Joseph was born on a cold winter day on December 23, 1805. He was the fifth of eleven children born to Joseph Smith, Sr., and Lucy Mack Smith.

Joseph's parents learned early-on that their son was an especially brave young man. When Joseph was seven years old, he needed to have a very painful operation to remove a piece of infected bone from his leg. If the operation were not performed, the doctor said, Joseph would soon have to have his whole leg removed.

There was no anesthetic to deaden the pain or put Joseph to sleep while the doctor worked. As they prepared for the surgery, the doctor told Joseph's mother, "Bring some rope. We can tie

South Royalton, Vermont, a typical New England village similar to Sharon, Vermont, birthplace of Joseph Smith, Jr. Photograph by George E. Anderson, 1912.

him down to the bedstead. And bring some brandy or wine; the pain will be almost unbearable." But little Joseph refused the strong drinks and said he would not need to be tied down with rope. "I will have my father sit on the bed and hold me in his arms," he said. Then Joseph asked his worried mother to leave the room and go outside so she wouldn't hear him cry out during the operation. "The Lord will help me," he told her. "I'll get through it."

The surgery was extremely painful, but Joseph held tight to his father. Lucy listened to Joseph's screams from outside, praying constantly that all would go well for her son. Lucy's prayers were answered. The surgery was a success, and Joseph's leg was able to heal, though he walked with a slight limp for the rest of his life.

The Smiths were farmers, and young Joseph enjoyed working out in the fields alongside his brothers and sisters. But farming was difficult in Vermont. The soil was rocky, and sometimes there was a frost every month of the year. As Joseph's father held a few tiny ears of corn from their garden in his hand, frozen from a July snowstorm, he decided to move the family to Palmyra, New York. The future prophet was ten years old.

There, in New York, the whole family worked hard to pay for their new farmland. Joseph, Sr., taught school while his wife Lucy sold painted tablecloths, root beer, bread and pies to neighbors and those passing through town. The Smith children cleared the land for planting, tapped sugar maple trees for syrup, and worked for other farmers.

As young Joseph chopped wood and plowed fields, his muscles hardened, and he grew to be tall for his age. He was strong and healthy, despite his limp. Farmers were eager to hire him because he was an especially hard worker. And, even after a long day of work in the hot sun, Joseph kept his happy disposition. He was known as "a clever, jovial boy."

After chores were done, Joseph loved to participate in homemade sports like wrestling, games with a ball, and horseback riding. One of his favorite games was called "pulling sticks," a contest in which two people sat on the ground facing each other, with the soles of their feet together. They pulled on a large stick they held between them until one person was pulled to an upright position.

But there was more to Joseph's life than working the soil and having fun. The Smith family prayed together each morning and evening, enjoyed singing hymns, and read the Bible together. Religion was important to Joseph. But the churches of his day raised more questions in Joseph's mind than they answered. Preachers from the various churches were trying to win converts. "Come here—we have the truth," one seemed to say. "No, come over here, we have the truth," another would call out. Even the Smith family could not agree on which Church to join. Everyone seemed to have a different opinion. The more young Joseph listened, the more confused he became.

Joseph, now fourteen, turned to the family Bible for help. One verse of scripture caught his attention more than any other: "If any of you lack wisdom, let him ask of God, that giveth to all men liberally . . . and it shall be given him." (James 1:5.) Could it be that Heavenly Father would help him answer his questions? Joseph decided to find out.

In the spring of 1820, Joseph walked into the countryside near his home to a beautiful grove of trees where he could be alone to pray. He had never prayed aloud before but decided this time he should. He had an especially important question. Joseph knelt and began to pray. Shortly after he began, he received an astonishing answer, which he described:

> I saw a pillar of light exactly over my head, above the brightness of the sun, which descended gradually until it fell upon me. . . . When the light rested upon me I saw two Personages, whose brightness and glory defy all description, standing above me in the air. One of them spake unto me, calling me by name and said, pointing to the other—*This is My Beloved Son. Hear Him!* (Joseph Smith—History 1:16–17.)

Filled with wonder and awe, Joseph realized that God the Father stood before him, and at his side was his Son Jesus Christ. The Savior spoke to Joseph, saying that his sins had been for-

The Sacred Grove on the Joseph Smith, Sr., farm, near Palmyra village, New York. Photograph by George E. Anderson, ca. 1912.

given. In answer to Joseph's question about which church he should join, the Savior instructed Joseph to join none of them, for they had strayed from the gospel; "their hearts are far from me," he said. (Joseph Smith—History 1:19.)

No one knows how long Joseph talked with the Savior, but all too soon the pillar of light began to diminish, and the heavenly beings left. Joseph was filled with peace, joy, and happiness. He returned home physically weak, but his spirit was soaring higher than the birds that flew overhead.

As he entered the house, his mother could tell something was different about her son. "Joseph," she asked, "are you ill?"

"I am well enough," he answered. Then he explained: "I have learned for myself that the true church is not yet on the earth."

Joseph's mother and the rest of the Smith family gathered around and listened intently as he described what had happened in the grove. They knew Joseph was a truthful boy and believed what he told them about the vision he had seen.

But they soon found out that hardly anybody else did. Neighbors teased young Joseph and insisted he had made up the whole story. Ministers laughed, saying it was utter nonsense to think God the Father and Jesus Christ would appear to a fourteen-year-old farm boy. How frustrating this was for Joseph! He wrote: "I had seen a vision; I knew it, and I knew that God knew it, and I could not deny it, neither dared I do it; at least I knew that by so doing I would offend God." (Joseph Smith–History 1:25.)

Joseph's experiences with heavenly beings were only beginning. On the night of September 21, 1823, when Joseph was seventeen, while he was praying to his Heavenly Father, he noticed that a light began to fill his bedroom until it shone brighter than the sun at noonday. An angel appeared in the midst of the light, standing above the floor. Joseph recalled: "He had on a loose robe of most exquisite whiteness. It was a whiteness beyond anything earthly I had ever seen. . . . His whole person was glorious beyond description, and his countenance truly like lightning." (Joseph Smith–History 1:31–32.)

Joseph watched in wide-eyed wonderment as the personage moved toward him without touching the floor. Then the heavenly visitor spoke, calling Joseph by name, saying he was Moroni, a messenger sent by God. The angel went on to say that Heavenly Father had an important work for Joseph to do. He was to bring forth a book buried in a hill close by, an ancient record engraved upon plates of gold. The plates contained a history of nations that had previously existed on the American continent. The fullness of the everlasting gospel was contained in the book, as given by the Savior to the ancient people in America.

Joseph was spellbound. He listened to the angel tell how, when the right time came, he—a poor farm boy—would be able to translate the ancient writing on the plates of gold. He would have the help of the Lord and two small stones called the Urim and Thummim.

Moroni told Joseph many other marvelous things, but finally the light began to diminish, and Moroni disappeared. He returned to Joseph's bedside two more times during the night, each time repeating the message he had given during the first visit and adding more. Moroni warned Joseph that Satan would tempt him to sell the gold plates for a great amount of money. But the record was sacred and would be withheld from him if he tried to use it for anything except to glorify God and build his kingdom.

Immediately after Moroni left the third time, Joseph heard the rooster crow in the yard. It was morning—the angelic visits had lasted the whole night. Joseph could hardly comprehend what had happened. The Lord had chosen him to be a prophet! Joseph was to play an important role in preparing for the second coming of Christ to the earth.

This was a time of mixed feelings for Joseph. He felt thrilled and in awe of the visions he had seen. He was humbled to know that Heavenly Father had chosen him for such an important calling. And yet, Joseph also said, "I do not wish to be a great deal better than anybody else." He often reminded himself and others that the Lord had chosen "a weak thing" to accomplish his work on the earth.

In 1827, the angel Moroni gave Joseph permission to take the plates from their hiding place in the hill (today called the Hill Cumorah). Joseph was twenty-one years old and now had a wife. Earlier that year he had married tall, dark-haired Emma Hale.

Emma drove in a horse-drawn wagon to the Hill Cumorah with Joseph the night he obtained the golden plates. Joseph was filled with wonder as he saw by moonlight the glitter of the gold plates inside a box made of stones cemented together. He ran his fingers over the curious markings on the ancient records.

Fearful that somebody might try to steal the plates because of their great monetary worth, Joseph hid them first in an old log in the woods, and later in a specially built cherry-wood box that he buried under the hearthstones in his father's home. Joseph was now responsible for the plates, and he was prepared to guard them with his very life, if need be.

And guard them he did. Word soon spread that Joseph had found a "gold bible." Immediately people from the surrounding countryside began to snoop and harass him with questions. Visitors stopped by at all hours to see the golden plates, but Joseph said they could not see them. He had been commanded by an angel not to show them to anyone without permission.

Emma Hale Smith, wife of Joseph Smith, Jr. Portrait artist unknown.

Many insisted and offered money and property to see the plates, but Joseph was faithful to his promise to protect the sacred record. For this, he and his family were persecuted and abused.

This trouble caused Joseph and Emma to move to Harmony, Pennsylvania, hiding the plates in a barrel of beans for protection along the way. There, in a more peaceful setting, Joseph began translating the plates. During the next three years, Joseph translated the scriptures by reading them aloud, often from behind a curtain, to a scribe.

By March 1830, the Book of Mormon had been completely translated, delivered to a publisher, and printed, bound and ready for sale. It was a happy day for Joseph! In the coming years, millions of copies of this sacred record would be printed, and future generations of Latter-day Saints would be called upon by their leaders to "flood the earth with the Book of Mormon."

Joseph continued to have sacred experiences. The angel John the Baptist visited him and his close friend Oliver Cowdery on the banks of the Susquehanna River and conferred the Aaronic Priesthood upon them. In a similar manner, a short time later, the ancient apostles Peter, James and John gave the Melchizedek Priesthood to Joseph and Oliver.

On April 6, 1830, the Lord instructed Joseph to organize the Church of Jesus Christ. Several baptisms were performed that day, including those of the Prophet's parents, whom he dearly loved. After baptizing his father, the Prophet Joseph stood upon the shore and, taking his father by the hand, said with tears of joy, "Oh, my God! I have lived to see my own father baptized into the true Church of Jesus Christ!"

The stage was now set for the gospel to go forth to all the world. As the Church grew, Joseph prayed continually that he would be worthy to be the Lord's prophet. Joseph wrote in his diary: "Oh may God grant that I may be directed in all my thoughts," and "O Lord, fill [my] heart with wisdom and understanding."

Joseph was commanded by the Lord to move over one hundred fifty Latter-day Saints to Kirtland, Ohio, in the early spring of 1831. Kirtland was to have a great influence on Joseph and the Church. There he received the Word of Wisdom revelation for the Church. There, at great sacrifice, the Church members built a sacred temple in which the Saints would receive many spiritual blessings. There in the Kirtland Temple Joseph again saw the Savior as well as the ancient prophets Moses, Elias, and Elijah. Those heavenly messengers strengthened Joseph's faith, gave him important priesthood authority, and filled him with courage to face the trials that were soon to come.

The Church grew rapidly, but persecution of the Saints increased and became more brutal. Joseph himself did not escape the violent attacks. On March 24, 1832, an angry crowd of men broke into the home where he was staying, dragged him outside, and carried him to a lonely meadow. There they beat him, stripped off his clothes, and covered him with tar and feathers. They tried to force a bottle of poison into his mouth, but Joseph broke the vial with his teeth, chipping a front tooth. Finally they choked him until he was unconscious and left him for dead.

After waking up, Joseph found help at a nearby farmhouse. During the night, friends carefully removed the tar. But Joseph did not allow even this awful experience to stop his work. He preached a sermon the very next morning and baptized three converts.

The beatings were painful, but Joseph was most deeply hurt when some of his closest friends turned against him. His friends meant so much to him. Yet he carried his sorrows and burdens with courage and prayed for those who lost their testimonies of the gospel.

It soon became necessary to move again, and the Saints left their homes in Kirtland for Far West, Missouri. There it seemed that their troubles were even worse. Angry mobs, who wanted the Mormons out of their state, destroyed their businesses, burned many homes and crops, whipped and beat many of the leaders, destroyed their livestock and killed men, women, and children.

Joseph, his beloved older brother Hyrum, and several others were arrested and kept in the small, dark, and filthy Liberty Jail. Most of that time their feet were bound together in chains. Joseph was extremely lonesome during this time. He missed his wife and four children terribly. Joseph wrote to Emma:

> Oh, that I may have the privilege of seeing once more my lovely family, in the enjoyment of the sweets of liberty and social life. To press them to my bosom and kiss their lovely cheeks would fill my heart with unspeakable gratitude.

He also wrote special messages to his children:

> Tell them father loves them with a perfect love and he is doing all he can to get away from the mob to come to them. Tell little Joseph he must be a good boy. Father loves him with a perfect love. He is the eldest and must not hurt those that are smaller than him, but comfort them. Tell little Frederick father loves him with all his heart. He is a lovely boy. Julia is a lovely little girl. Love her also. She is a promising child. Tell her father wants her to remember him and be a good girl.

After nearly six months, with the help of a guard, Joseph and his friends escaped while being moved to another prison. Joseph joined the Saints who had now moved from Missouri to the area around Quincy, Illinois. What a happy reunion Joseph had with his family and friends!

But these were difficult times. The Saints had no homes, no land, no place to settle. Out of poverty and persecution, however, came new growth. Joseph led them to a lovely but swampy place on the banks of the Missouri River, named it Nauvoo, which means "beautiful location," and set them to draining the land and building again. As mayor of the new city, Joseph laid out a city plan that included wide streets and large lots for homes, schoolhouses, businesses, and a magnificent temple.

Joseph continued to build spiritually as well, receiving important revelations from the Lord. Many of these were added to the Doctrine and Covenants, which was earlier called the Book of Commandments.

This was Joseph's finest hour. His city flourished, the Church grew, and Joseph's human qualities made him a beloved leader. One friend said he was "kind and considerate, taking a personal interest in all people. He considered everyone his equal." Another said he was "very sociable, easy, cheerful, kind and hospitable—in a word, a jolly fellow."

Joseph took a special interest in children. He picked wildflowers for little girls, settled quarrels between schoolchildren, and gathered babies into his arms for a squeeze and a loving word. During the winter, he loved sliding on the ice with his own children and their friends. He took his family to musical concerts, the theater, circus performances, and on boat trips on the Mississippi River.

One pioneer wrote that as thousands of immigrants arrived from the eastern United States and from across the ocean:

> Joseph would make his way to as many of the wagons as he well could, and cordially shake the hand of each person. Every child and young babe in the company were especially noticed by him and tenderly taken by the hand, with his kind words and blessings. He loved innocence and purity

Part of Nauvoo, with the completed Nauvoo Temple on the bluff overlooking the city. Photographer unknown.

and seemed to find it in the greatest perfection with the
prattling child.

Once, while delivering a sermon at a cottage meeting, a little
girl became tired and sleepy and began to cry. Joseph stopped
speaking, sat down on a bench behind him, and motioned to
her to come to him. He put her on his lap and patted her, and
she went off to sleep while he completed his sermon.

No doubt about it. The Lord had chosen a loving, caring
man to be the prophet of the Restoration.

The Saints admired these qualities in Joseph. So many of
the other religious leaders of this time were long-faced and stern.
They frowned upon dancing, playing an instrument, or participating in sports. But the Prophet Joseph Smith could be both
serious and playful, spiritual and full of laughter, reverent and
also happy. He enjoyed life and taught the Saints to do the same,
in spite of their trials and problems.

The Saints lived in peace for a short time in Nauvoo, but
soon the old persecutions began to arise again. In June of 1844,
following much anti-Mormon violence, Joseph and Hyrum said
good-bye to their families and friends and surrendered to the
Illinois authorities to answer in court the false charges brought
against them.

The governor of Illinois promised Joseph that they would be
protected. Joseph wrote a last letter to Emma from a cell in
Carthage Jail: "I am resigned to my lot, knowing I am justified,
and have done the best that could be done. Give my love to the
children and all my friends."

On the afternoon of June 27, a mob made up of members
of the Illinois militia blackened their faces and headed for Carthage Jail. The jail guards, who were part of the plot, fired upon
the mob only with blanks. The guards only pretended to protect

Carthage Jail, where Joseph and Hyrum Smith were martyred and John Taylor seriously wounded. Engraving by Charles B. Hall.

their well-known prisoners. A small group of the mob with loaded guns stormed up the stairs of the jail and burst into the room, firing upon Joseph, Hyrum, John Taylor, and Willard Richards.

Almost instantly, Joseph and Hyrum were killed, and John Taylor was seriously wounded. Crying out, "Oh Lord, my God!" Joseph fell through a window onto the ground below, at the feet of the rest of the mob.

No day in the history of the Church has been sadder. It was

Joseph Smith, Jr. Photograph by C. W. Carter, ca. 1880, of painting by unknown artist.

as if time stood still and the earth stopped turning. All sound and movement ceased. Joseph the Prophet was dead. Joseph the husband, father, and friend was gone.

The bodies of Joseph and Hyrum were brought back to Nauvoo in two wagons by their brother Samuel to their sorrowing families. There, thousands of Saints wept at the deaths of the Prophet and his brother. The news of their murders hit Nauvoo and the nearby communities of Saints "like a thunderbolt, crushing the people to the earth," one woman wrote. Another said, "How lonely was the feeling! How cold, barren and desolate! [Joseph] had spoken for the last time on earth." For many early pioneers, knowing the Prophet Joseph Smith had been the greatest blessing in their lives.

Joseph and Hyrum were secretly buried in the basement of an unfinished hotel, the Nauvoo House. They were later moved and buried on a lot near Joseph and Emma's first home in Nauvoo, where they rest to this day.

Joseph Smith's life on earth was shorter than any other latter-day prophet—thirty-eight years. But in those few years, the scriptures tell us, he did more for the salvation of men in this world "than any other man who ever lived in it," save Jesus only. (D&C 135:3.) Joseph's work on the earth was mightily finished, and the Lord's work had mightily begun.

Brigham Young

A Barefoot Boy from Vermont

Thirteen-year-old John Henry Seely was excited after hearing the announcement made in the small meetinghouse in Mt. Pleasant, Utah. "Brothers and Sisters," the bishop began, "I'm pleased to tell you we will soon be having a special visitor to our community. Brother Brigham has sent word that he will arrive here later this week. Let every citizen of Mt. Pleasant do what he or she can to make our town presentable to the prophet of the Lord."

Everyone was thrilled and spent that week in September 1868 tidying up their homes, yards, and farms for a visit from President Brigham Young. The bishop assigned John and his boyhood pals to move away the large rocks from the main road in Mt. Pleasant, making the pathway clear for President Young's caravan. With each large stone he carried to the side of the road, John imagined seeing the famous leader.

Brigham Young, or "Brother Brigham" as the Saints called him, had been president of the Church since 1847—three years after Joseph Smith was murdered. John Seely's parents had crossed the plains in 1847 with Brother Brigham and had learned to love and respect the rugged, hard-working colonizer. Some had even compared him to the ancient prophet Moses, leading his people away from persecution to a promised land where they could worship in peace. The people of Mt. Pleasant could not have been more excited about the prophet's visit if they had been expecting the king of England instead.

On the day of President Young's arrival, the Mount Pleasant Brass Band met him and his party of nearly thirty carriages and escorted the group into town, announcing their triumphal entry with lively marching tunes. The street was lined with Sunday School children dressed in their best. Men waved their hats enthusiastically and others held large banners saying "Lion of the Lord," "Defender of Right," or "Welcome!" It was the biggest event of the year.

Brother Brigham led the procession in a simple but well-built buggy (he didn't care for the frills and fringe that often decorated other carriages). As John Seely saw President Young approaching, he carefully studied the Prophet's appearance. What he saw was a handsome, portly gentleman with thick, wavy, nearly-white hair and a trimmed beard. He had radiant blue eyes, a square set jaw, and a pleasant expression on his face. President Young wore a large green wool cape to keep the dust off his clothes, short pull-on boots, and a straw hat. He seemed grand-fatherly, warm and friendly.

Later that night, President Young received visitors in front of a warm crackling fire at the home of one of the local leaders. Still watching the prophet, John noticed that Brother Brigham paid special attention to the children—listening to their questions, hearing their stories, and giving them marbles. The friendly atmosphere reminded one of the president's traveling companions to share a funny story with those in the room. He told of a similar visit to another community when President Young stopped at the home of Anson Call, a pioneer:

Brigham Young, about age sixty. Photograph by C. W. Carter, ca. 1861

Sitting in a circle around the fireplace, Brigham invited Anson's little daughter to sit on his knee. During a lull in the conversation, he reached out and turned her head so he could look her full in the face. He started to tell her how pretty she was when she blurted out, "Your eyes look just like our sow's!" Anson was embarrassed, but Brigham took the child by the hand and headed for the door. "Take me to the pig pen. I want to see this pig that has eyes just like mine."

Brother Brigham enjoyed the retelling of the story as much as anyone and joined in the hearty laughter afterwards. Those who were there would long remember his visit to Mt. Pleasant. Certainly, John Henry Seeley never forgot seeing the Lord's prophet.

Brigham Young is probably the most well-known Latter-day Saint in the history of the Church. But his life did not start out as if he were destined to become one of the greatest colonizers and religious leaders in United States history. In fact, life started out cold and hungry for the future prophet.

Brigham Young was born on June 1, 1801, in Whitingham, Vermont, the ninth of eleven children. His mother, Abigail (Nabby) Howe Young, was ill with tuberculosis during Brigham's infancy, and he was more or less reared by his thirteen-year-old sister, Fanny. "Briggie," as he was called, became so attached to Fanny that she had to carry him on her hip even when she milked the cow.

John Young, Brigham's father, had fought in the Revolutionary War under General George Washington himself. John walked over a hundred miles home when that war ended, carrying a cannonball all the way. He was a stern, strict man who didn't allow his children to dance, listen to the sound of a violin, or walk more than half an hour on Sunday. Brigham quickly decided that this was not the way he wanted to raise his own children. He said:

> I shall not subject my little children to such a course of unnatural training, but they shall go to the dance, study music, read novels, and do anything else that will tend to expand their frames, add fire to their spirits, improve their minds and make them feel free and un-trammeled in body and mind.

When Brigham was three years old, the Young family moved to Chenango County, New York. By the time Brigham was eight, he took care of many household chores because his mother's tuberculosis had slowly worsened. He made bread, churned butter, and made most of the family meals. Brigham tenderly cared for his mother as she lay ill in bed. Each morning he carried her from the bed to the table and then to a chair in front of the fireplace before going out to work for the day.

The Young family, which included eleven children, was very poor. Brigham rarely had enough to eat or sufficient clothes to protect himself from the weather. "I had to plow in the midst of roots barefooted and if I had on a pair of pants that would cover me I did pretty well." Brigham owned just one pair of shoes during his boyhood. He used them only for church. Even then, he carried them in his hands until he reached the church lot, taking them off again after the service before he walked home.

During the cold New York winters, Brigham worked with "insufficient food until my stomach would ache." Once, he and his younger brother Lorenzo were left alone at home for two days without any food. Brigham grabbed his father's musket, killed a robin, skinned and cleaned it, and cooked it for an evening stew.

When Brigham was fourteen years old, his mother died. The children were "farmed out" to live with relatives, and Brigham missed being with his brothers and sisters.

Brigham was soon old enough to learn a trade. He wanted to learn how to make things with his hands and became an apprentice to a carpenter in Auburn, New York. He proved to have great talent and went into business for himself making beautiful chairs, beds, and cabinets. He also made brooms, fireplace mantels, and spinning wheels. Brigham became famous in his community as a talented glazier (a person who designs and makes windows). He was known for the beauty of his stairwell decorations, fanlight doorways, and attic windows.

When he was twenty-three, Brigham married Miriam Works and moved to Mendon, New York. There, he built a carpentry shop next to the Cayuga Brook, a large millstream. Waterpower from the stream turned a wooden wheel and gave power to the lathe.

But even now, with a wife he loved and a valuable trade, there was still something missing in Brigham's life. He wanted religion . . . but not just any religion.

Brigham had studied the Bible daily as a young boy and became convinced that the religion he was seeking should make people *happy*. Brigham still felt uncomfortable about his own stern, strict childhood.

While searching for answers, Brigham attended several different churches and found that most of their members had long, sad faces. He was disgusted to find people who attended church on Sunday and then cheated their neighbors in business dealings the very next day. He was grateful that his parents had taught him to be strictly honest, to return items to neighbors—even as small as a pin.

Brigham also believed in prophets, apostles, baptism by immersion, and free agency. In 1830, when he was twenty-eight years old, he found these principles and much more when he was given his first copy of the Book of Mormon. Brigham was a careful, thoughtful student and for two years studied this new volume of scripture. He did not want to rush into something as important as this. He described his attitudes by saying:

> Wait a little while; what is the doctrine of the book, and of the revelations the Lord has given? Let me apply my heart to them; and after I had done this, I consider it to be my right to know for myself, as much as any man on earth.

Brigham became excited about what he was reading, and the spirit of the Holy Ghost burned like a fire within him:

> I knew it was true, as well as I knew that I could see with my eyes, or feel by the touch of my fingers. . . . Had not this been the case, I never would have embraced it to this day. . . . I wished [to have enough time] to prove all things for myself.

Brigham was baptized April 14, 1832, in his own mill stream and was ordained an elder the same day while his clothes were still wet. A month later his wife was also baptized. Brigham's excitement and love for the Church and its teachings never wavered even a minute the rest of his life. Brigham had found the truth and he rejoiced!

However, during the same year as his baptism—one of the happiest events of his life—came also a very sad experience: his wife of seven years died, leaving Brigham with two small daughters.

Brigham decided it was time for a big change. After finding a loving couple to temporarily care for his two daughters, Brigham set out to preach the gospel and bear his testimony to others. He called himself on a mission, so to speak. Brigham locked up his carpentry shop and bid his customers good-bye. He was starting a new life—one completely dedicated to the Lord.

Brigham's first order of business was to travel to Kirtland, Ohio, to meet the Prophet Joseph Smith. Brigham found Joseph out chopping wood:

> Here my joy was full at the privilege of shaking the hand of the Prophet of God, and receiving the sure testimony, by the spirit of prophecy, that he was all that any man could believe him to be as a true Prophet.

Brigham became one of Joseph Smith's most loyal and trusted friends. He would later say: "I feel like shouting *Hallelujah,* all the time, when I think that I ever knew Joseph Smith."

In 1835, Brigham moved to Kirtland and was ordained an apostle by Joseph Smith. By now he had married his second wife, Mary Ann Angel, and he was happily reunited with his two daughters.

At this time trouble was brewing within the Church. Many Saints began to lose faith in Joseph and even talked of replacing him with another prophet of their own choosing. But not Brigham. In a tense meeting with many of Joseph's critics, held in the Kirtland Temple, Brigham stood up and defended the Prophet with all his might:

> I told them that Joseph was a Prophet, and I knew it, and they might rail and slander him as much as they pleased. [But] they could not destroy the appointment of the Prophet of God. I stood close by Joseph and with all the wisdom and power God bestowed upon me, put forth my utmost energies to unite the quorums of the Church.

As a result of these troubles, nearly eleven thousand Latter-day Saints left Kirtland, Ohio, and settled in various places in Missouri. But it wasn't long before they had to move on again. Angry mobs drove them from Missouri. Joseph Smith had been arrested on false charges and was in jail when the Saints needed to be moved.

Joseph assigned Brigham the difficult task of moving the Saints out of Missouri and across the Mississippi River. The move, which took place in the middle of winter, was difficult and dangerous. Many of the Saints were ill or suffered frostbite. Brigham's own infant daughter was thrown from a wagon and run over. She miraculously survived.

Brigham served a mission to England in 1839. Just getting there turned out to be a powerful, humbling experience. Not only was he very ill when he left home, but his voyage across the Atlantic Ocean also brought him to his knees in sickness, and he spent much of the time in mighty prayer:

> I was very sick in my head and stomach. I felt as though I could not endure many such voyages. Were it not for the power of God and his tender mercy I should despair. But the Lord is my strength. When the winds were contrary, the Twelve (Apostles) agreed to ask Him to calm the seas and give us a fair wind. We did so and the wind immediately changed and from that time on it has blown in our favor.

Even under the most difficult circumstances, Brigham's testimony of the gospel never wavered. He knew it was true.

Brigham's service to the Church was just beginning. He later said, "No summer passed over my head but what I was traveling and preaching. And the only thing I ever received from the Church or the Prophet was in 1842, when Brother Joseph gave me the half of a small pig that the brethren had brought to him."

But Brigham knew the rewards of serving the Lord were far greater than any money could bring. "I just do the thing that I know to be right and the Lord blesses me."

Brigham was away on another mission in New England when the Prophet Joseph was murdered in Carthage Jail in Illinois on June 27, 1844. When Brigham received word of the Prophet's death, his eyes filled with tears. An angry mob had robbed the world of one of its choicest spirits.

Brigham immediately returned to Nauvoo. He was now deeply concerned about the future of the Church. It wasn't completely clear to the Latter-day Saints who should succeed Joseph as president of the Church. Several men claimed that they should now be in charge.

Brigham knew the priesthood authority to lead the Church rested with the Quorum of the Twelve Apostles. Joseph himself had laid his hands on their heads before his death and given them "the keys of the kingdom." As president of the Quorum, Brigham knew he held the keys and powers to now receive direction from the Lord. But how would he convince the people?

When Brigham stood to speak before a large gathering of Saints in Nauvoo on August 8 (forty days after Joseph's death), an event took place that those who saw considered to be a miracle. A young man, Benjamin Johnson, was standing near the front and described what happened:

> As soon as Brigham spoke I jumped upon my feet, for in every possible degree it was Joseph's voice, and his person, in look, attitude, dress and appearance; [it] was Joseph himself, personified; and I knew in a moment the spirit and mantle of Joseph was upon him.

Wilford Woodruff, who was also in the audience, wrote: "If

Brigham Young, about age forty-four, approximately one year after Joseph Smith's death. Photographer unknown.

I had not seen him with my own eyes, there is no one that could have convinced me that it was not Joseph Smith."

This experience convinced many that Brigham Young was the Lord's choice to be their new prophet.

These were trying times. The Saints continued to suffer persecutions. Anti-Mormon feelings ran high. As life became more difficult and dangerous for the Latter-day Saints, the spirit whispered to Brigham that they should leave Nauvoo as fast as they could.

Now the Lord needed a man to accomplish what seemed to be utterly impossible: to move sixteen thousand Saints out of Nauvoo and across the Mississippi River and get them safely across the plains to a new home somewhere in the West fifteen hundred miles away. Only a leader whom the people would respect and follow, who knew how to organize, inspire, and encourage the Saints could accomplish such a task. That leader would have to be fearless and not easily discouraged. When the Lord needed such a leader, Brigham Young was ready.

What followed was the greatest western migration of settlers in United States history. Brigham called on blacksmiths, carpenters, and mechanics to work day and night making wagons for the long journey. Brigham instructed the Saints to buy teams of horses and oxen and to load their wagons with food, cooking pots and pans, blankets, plows, and tools.

The Saints moved from Nauvoo to Winter Quarters (now Florence), Nebraska, in 1846. Then in 1847, the first small group of pioneers began the one-thousand-mile journey to the Salt Lake Valley—led by their "Moses," Brigham Young. As the first wagon train pulled out, Brigham did not just sit in a comfortable, sheltered wagon whistling happy tunes. A camp historian wrote: "He was out in the rain all day arranging the wagons, pitching tents, chopping wood and so on—until all were

Brigham Young, about age fifty-one.

comfortable." At seven o'clock the next morning, Brigham "shouldered his axe and walked to the creek, where he was engaged at chopping and raising a bridge till eleven."

As the journey progressed, Brigham scurried from camp to camp in his buggy attending to hundreds of details each day—settling quarrels, repairing wagon wheels, blessing the sick, and making sure the Saints were having their evening prayers. If the pioneers' cattle began straying off toward a buffalo herd, Brigham was one of the first to jump on a horse and bring them back. If some in the group were, in Brigham's opinion, wasting time by playing cards and dominoes, he didn't hesitate to tell them to repent and use their time more wisely! Above all, Brigham tried to lift their spirits as the Saints tried to get used to the endless walking, little sleep, and the constant dangers of un-friendly Indians and wild animals. One traveler wrote that the wolves "were so bold they would come right into camp and some put their feet on the wagon tongues and sniff in at the end of the wagon."

At the end of a long day, while sitting around the campfire, some of the pioneers would ask Brigham, "How will we know when we arrive at our destination since none of us, including you, have ever been there before?"

Brigham would calmly reply: "Oh, I will know it when I see it. We shall continue to travel the way the Spirit of the Lord directs us. The Lord has reserved for us a good place in the mountains and he will lead us directly to it." He said it with complete confidence, because he knew it was true.

Three-and-a-half months after beginning their trek, the tired but joyful pioneers entered the Salt Lake Valley—on July 24, 1847. Brigham, who had become very ill with Colorado tick fever, sat up from his bed in the back of Wilford Woodruff's wagon and looked out over the valley. He paused for a few

Great Salt Lake Valley, July 1847, when the first Saints arrived. Engraving by Charles B. Hall, based on a painting by H. L. A. Culmer.

minutes as if enwrapped in a vision, and then made his famous statement: "It is enough. This is the right place. Drive on."

For the next thirty years, Brigham worked tirelessly to build up the kingdom of God. He chose a site for a temple, directed the planting of crops, and had the future city surveyed and laid out into ten-acre blocks—each of which was divided into eight building lots. Land was carefully set aside for farms, schools, and parks.

Brigham later returned to the midwest and accompanied other groups of pioneers to the Valley. He started the Perpetual Emigration Fund, which raised money to help bring more than seventy-five thousand converts from other countries to Utah.

With the help of many other devoted, talented members of
the Church, President Young presided over the beginnings of
the Sunday School, the Primary organization for children, the
Retrenchment Society (which later became the Young Women's
program), and the reorganizing of the Relief Society, which began
in Nauvoo. Hundreds of meetinghouses were built throughout
the west, and missionaries were sent to preach the gospel in
countries all over the world. The Church grew, and the desert
began to "blossom like a rose."

President Young laid the cornerstone of the Salt Lake Temple,
dedicated the St. George Temple, had theaters built for the enjoyment of plays and operas, and saw to it that schoolhouses
were built to educate the children.

In addition to being the president of the Church, Brigham
Young served two four-year terms as governor of the Territory
of Utah. He encouraged the settlers to work together to build
railroads, dig canals, build fences, and construct roads. Grist
mills produced flour from their grain, and cotton and woolen
mills hummed continuously. During this time more than three
hundred settlements were established throughout the territory.
No wonder Utah became known as the "Beehive State"—everyone was busy as bees!

President Young knew recreation made people happy, and
his favorite activity was dancing—especially the cotillion, min-
uet, and square dances. He didn't approve of the waltz. When
asked why he liked to dance, he replied, "Besides my own [prob-
lems] I have the whole people's burdens, and I get rid of them
by kicking them off my toes."

Brigham went to great lengths to provide a happy, healthy
home for his family, most of whom lived in the Beehive House
and Lion House just east of Temple Square. He had sixteen
wives by whom he had fifty-seven children. In the Lion House,

Eagle Gate at the intersection of State Street and South Temple Street, with the Beehive House to the left. Photographer unknown.

The Lion House (left), Brigham Young's territorial offices (center), and the Beehive House (right). Photograph by Edward Martin, ca. 1862.

he had a children's recreation room built that contained ladders to climb, jumping ropes, roller skates, swings, and wooden swords. Teachers were brought in to teach his children gymnastics, fencing, and dancing.

A large garden and orchard behind the homes provided most of the food for family meals. In autumn the ripened fruit on the trees proved too tempting to the children. A high fence, built to keep children outside and fruit inside, even failed to solve the problem. So President Young got a big, bald eagle who seemed to realize it was his duty to patrol the garden. The eagle proved to be a very effective guard.

Daily chores kept the Young children busy and taught them the value of work. Clarissa Young, one of Brigham's daughters, described one little job she had which she *loved:*

> The family used to eat an early breakfast, but I always waited until ten o'clock when Father had his, so that I might be served with him. In those days he wore quite a long beard, and it was my duty to tie a bib over it in order to protect it from stray crumbs. I suppose one of the reasons why I enjoyed having my breakfast with Father was because he always had the things I liked. There was corn-meal mush and milk, hot doughnuts and syrup, codfish gravy, squabs [young pigeons] from the pigeon house, and some little delicacy from our own garden [such as strawberries or melons].

In the evenings after dinner, a family home evening was held, which included discussion of family problems, singing, and a program of the children reciting poems, playing instruments, and performing skits. At the end of the program, everyone knelt while Brigham offered the evening prayer. After the younger children were put to bed, the wives and older children made

Brigham Young, about age seventy-five. Photograph by C. R. Savage, ca. 1876.

popcorn or molasses candy for a bedtime treat. Brigham often enjoyed a bowl of fresh popped corn with sugar and cream.

So this was Brigham Young—a carpenter, painter, missionary, a trusted friend to Joseph Smith. He was a great colonizer, a tireless missionary, and a doting father. He loved dancing, good food, and the gospel.

Brigham's face could be aflame with anger at someone who dared call Joseph Smith a false prophet, or he could enjoy a hearty laugh after a child said his eyes looked just like a sow's. Brigham was tough enough to wade in icy water up to his chest to get a wagon through a raging river but tender-hearted enough to delight in having a small daughter tie a bib around his neck before breakfast.

When Brigham died on August 29, 1877, in his home in Salt Lake City, the Church as well as the state of Utah suffered a great loss. Several thousand people attended his funeral, then he was buried in a small, peaceful cemetery on First Avenue in Salt Lake City.

For being a barefoot boy from Vermont, Brigham Young had come a long, long way.

West side of Main Street, Salt Lake City. Photograph by C. W. Carter, 1868.

John Taylor

A Proper English Gentleman

The captain and sailors of the British ship were terrified. They had left England to sail for America just a few hours earlier and were in the English Channel when they suddenly ran into a dangerous storm. Strong winds blew against the ship, rocking it dangerously from side to side. High waves crashed against the sides, spilling water onto the deck where the crew worked desperately to keep the ship from sinking.

Passing several wrecked ships in the Channel, the crew and passengers became even more frightened as the noise of the surf got louder and they caught glimpses of the dangerous, rocky shoreline. Everyone on board feared for their lives, afraid that at any moment the waves would break the ship apart. Everyone, that is, except one passenger. His name was John Taylor.

John was a relatively young man—twenty-three years old. He was traveling alone and had never been on a ship before. Still, he was calm and unafraid in the midst of this terrible storm.

As John stood on the deck, he was reassured by a still, small voice that whispered, "You must yet go to America and preach the gospel." He later wrote, "As I stood amidst the raging elements, I felt as calm as though I was sitting in a parlor at home.

I believed I should reach America and perform my work."
John Taylor knew the Lord had something important for
him to do in America, and nothing was going to stop him—
especially not a ridiculous storm!

Soon, the storm ended, and a few weeks later the ship
sailed safely into New York harbor. John Taylor was a man
who had great faith and courage—in the face of many kinds
of storms. His story begins in England.

John Taylor was born on November 1, 1808, in a small
market town called Milnthorpe along the River Kent in
northern England. It was a wild and beautiful area with high
mountains, waterfalls, and lush green valleys.

John's parents, Agnes and James, saw to it that their ten
children studied the Bible each day and attended church regu-
larly. When John was a month old, his parents took him to the
nearby Heversham Parish Church where he was christened
and blessed to "keep God's holy laws and commandments."

But John was taught to be afraid of Heavenly Father, rather
than to feel loved by him. Once, when a mischievous boy pulled
down a kite John was flying and tore it up, the future prophet
became very angry and said a word he shouldn't have. Suddenly
alarmed at what he had done, John left the kite and cried all the
way home, fearful that the Lord would *never* forgive him.

John's father worked for the British government, so the
family could afford the things they needed. John became well-
educated, was taught proper manners, and learned to dress
like an English gentleman.

The Taylor family lived for a time in Liverpool and later
moved to the village of Hale, where young John worked on a
family farm they inherited from an uncle. It was John's first
experience at plowing, planting seed, and raking hay. His favorite

Bridge End Farm, John Taylor's probable birthplace in Milnthorpe, England. Photographer unknown, 1973.

part of farm life was riding horses, even though he was frequently bucked off.

As with the other young people, John needed to learn a trade so he could earn a living. He studied barrel making and later became an apprentice to a woodworker. He was taught how to operate a lathe and make beautiful wooden furniture.

John was a religious young man. He prayed while working out in the fields each day and encouraged his friends to do the same. He grew close to his Heavenly Father during his teenage years and told his parents he sometimes heard the "sweet music of angelic choirs."

John had spiritual experiences that he did not understand at the time but that foretold future events in his life. For instance, while still a small boy, John saw a vision in which "an angel in heaven was holding a trumpet to his mouth, sounding a message to the nations." "What could it mean?" he asked himself.

John joined the Methodist Church in England when he was sixteen and a year later became a traveling minister. But still he felt there was something more God wanted him to do.

Once, while on his way to preach to a small group, John learned more clearly where he should perform his mission. He told a friend, "I have a strong impression on my mind that I have to go to America and preach the gospel." He knew very little about America except for what he had learned in school. John was puzzled as to why he should go there instead of staying in England to preach to his friends and neighbors.

But John's trust in the Lord was great. Six years later (in 1832) he made the voyage—which began so dangerously—to America. He joined his parents and four brothers and sisters who had traveled ahead of him and had settled near Toronto, Canada.

In Canada, John met two people who would change his life. The first was Leonora Cannon, a lovely Englishwoman, who became his wife. The second was a husky, black-haired Mormon missionary named Parley P. Pratt.

When the Taylors met Elder Pratt, he was an apostle of The Church of Jesus Christ of Latter-day Saints. Even though John was serving as a Methodist preacher, he and his wife felt strongly that their church did not have the complete truth. "This isn't the work the Lord sent me here to do," John said sadly to his wife. Something was still missing.

For three weeks, John followed Elder Pratt from place to place listening to him preach. He was determined to prove Elder Pratt wrong . . . or right. He wrote down his sermons and compared them to the Bible. John and Leonora also studied the Book of Mormon, which Elder Pratt had given them.

To their joy, after a great deal of study and prayer, John and Leonora knew that Elder Pratt was teaching the truth they had been searching for. They were baptized members of The Church of Jesus Christ of Latter-day Saints in May 1836.

John was not the type to give himself to anything half-heartedly. From this point on, he devoted his entire life to preaching the restored gospel and helping the Church. After being ordained an elder, he joined Elder Pratt, and they taught and baptized a great many people in Canada. His greatest thrill was being able to baptize his own parents, Agnes and James Taylor.

Many things had now become clearer to John. He now knew why the Lord had wanted him to leave England and come to America. He also knew the meaning of the vision he had received as a young boy. The angel had announced a message to the world, and John's heart had been ready to receive it. He was grateful he had listened to the Spirit and trusted in the Lord.

When John first met the Prophet Joseph Smith in Kirtland, Ohio, he felt "a charge like an electrical shock" when he shook his hand. He realized he had met a true prophet of God.

But all was not well in Kirtland. Partly because of the failure of several Church businesses, some of Joseph Smith's former friends turned against him. They criticized him in open meetings and claimed he was a fallen prophet. This angered John Taylor, and he became one of the Prophet's most faithful defenders. He later said:

John Taylor, age forty-four. Engraving by Fredrick Piercy, 1852.

I testify before God, angels and men, that Joseph Smith is a good, honorable, virtuous man, that his doctrines are good, scriptural, and wholesome. If I did not believe that Joseph Smith is a prophet, I would not be here.

After returning to Canada for a short time, John and Leonora received word from the Prophet Joseph Smith that he wanted them to join the Saints living in Ohio. "It won't be an easy move," John told his wife. The journey would cover twelve hundred miles, and they had very little money. But John made plans to leave and reassured his worried wife, "God will open out the way." John's faith was rewarded when a man named John Mills said he would travel with the Taylors and share his covered sleigh, wagons, teams, food, and clothing with them.

The Taylors arrived safely in Ohio, where John was called, by a revelation to Joseph Smith, to be an apostle. Upon receiving his call, he said:

> When I first entered upon Mormonism, I did it with my eyes open; I counted the cost. I looked upon it as a life-long job and I considered that I was not only enlisted for time, but for eternity and did not wish to shrink now, although I feel my incompetency.

John Taylor and other members of the Quorum of the Twelve Apostles were soon called on a mission to Great Britain. This mission was a great sacrifice for the Taylor family. John's wife and children lived in a twenty-foot square room in an abandoned army barracks in Iowa for the two years while he was away.

John became very sick as he left for his mission, but he knew the Lord would help him. On the way to New York, John was so weak from illness that he fainted along the roadside. His companion, Wilford Woodruff, found a doctor to help him, but John insisted that they continue their journey after resting for a few days. In New York City, John found he had only one cent in his pocket. But several people donated money to pay for his passage on the ship to England.

John served an excellent mission. He was proud to be able

to preach the gospel in his boyhood town of Liverpool, England. He was the first Mormon missionary to preach in Ireland, and he baptized the family of his wife's brother, George Cannon. He helped organize several hundred Saints who emigrated to the United States, and he set up branches of the Church in every major city in Great Britain.

When John and the other apostles returned from England on July 1, 1841, hundreds of Saints in Nauvoo gathered to welcome them home. Joseph Smith was the first to shake their hands.

John was an excellent writer, and Joseph Smith asked him to be the editor of the *Times and Seasons,* a newspaper printed by the Church. He also published a weekly newspaper called the *Nauvoo Neighbor.* In his articles, John continued to defend the Church and the Prophet Joseph Smith against criticism. He was nicknamed the "Defender of the Faith."

On June 27, 1844, tragedy struck, and John Taylor was there. Joseph and Hyrum were unfairly arrested and placed in Carthage Jail. John Taylor and another apostle, Willard Richards, stayed with the Smiths, saying, "We intend to do all we can to protect you."

Inside the small, secluded jail cell, Joseph Smith asked John to sing one of his favorite songs, "A Poor Wayfaring Man of Grief." John had a beautiful voice, and his singing comforted the Prophet.

Although these imprisoned men were promised protection, several dozen men, their faces painted black with axle grease, easily passed the guards at the front of the jailhouse. They raced up the wooden stairs and, firing their guns, burst into the room where the four Church leaders were being held.

The Prophet Joseph and Hyrum were shot and killed. A bullet hit John in the leg, and another hit his chest, striking his silver

John Taylor's silver pocket watch that stopped a bullet fired at Carthage Jail. Photographer unknown.

pocket watch, which was in his vest pocket. The watch saved his life by stopping a bullet that would have struck his heart. After John fell to the floor, three more bullets hit him.

When the mob saw that the Prophet Joseph was dead, they immediately fled. Willard Richards, a huge man weighing over three hundred pounds, was not hurt, and he covered John with a mattress for protection, then went to get help. John was later taken to his home in Nauvoo where he lay ill for many weeks. He had been badly hurt, but the Lord still had work for John to do, and he soon recovered.

Three years later, in 1847, the new president of the Church, Brigham Young, asked John Taylor to lead a group of more than fifteen hundred Saints across the plains. His group included 600 wagons, 124 horses, and 887 cows. They arrived in the Salt Lake Valley October 5, after traveling for more than three months. This was a demanding experience for an English gentleman who was used to having things neat and tidy.

John Taylor had a bright mind and a keen intellect, and the Church made good use of his talents. He served three more missions for the Church, returning again to England and, in 1849, serving in France and Germany. While in France, he directed the translation of the Book of Mormon into French and German. Later he presided over branches of the Church in the Eastern United States.

After John returned from his mission to the East, he remained in the Salt Lake Valley and was able to spend more time with his family. He had seven wives and thirty-five children. He especially enjoyed telling his children stories from Church history, letting them feel the bullet from the day he was nearly killed in Carthage Jail, which was still lodged under the skin of his left leg. The famous watch that saved his life is now in a museum.

John Taylor became the third president of the Church in 1880, after the death of Brigham Young. As president, he was concerned about the Church members who were especially poor. He once arranged for one thousand cows and five thousand sheep to be given to the poorest members who had lost their livestock during a severe winter. At this time, many Saints also owed money to the Church. They had had to borrow it to bring themselves to Utah from foreign countries. President Taylor erased half the debt they owed. It was a happy time for these people.

A careful dresser, President Taylor usually wore a dark suit

The First Presidency, 1880. President John Taylor is seated center. George Q. Cannon, first counselor, is to the left; Joseph F. Smith, second counselor, is to the right. Photographer unknown.

and highly polished boots, shined to perfection by one of his sons. He wore a red velvet coat on special occasions. He was often called "an English gentleman" because of his noble and courteous manner.

President Taylor's birthdays were always grand occasions for the whole family. An evening party was held, and General

Authorities were invited to enjoy the food, music, and dancing. One of his children wrote, "He was the king, and we were his princes and princesses."

President Taylor tended to be rather fussy about having things orderly and straight. Once, before leaving on a trip, he showed his sons how to plant the garden so the plants would be in straight, evenly spaced rows. He took great pride in his garden. After he left, the boys were in such a hurry to go and play with their friends that they planted by the "guess method." When President Taylor returned home a couple of weeks later and saw sprouts coming up in all sorts of odd places, he was silent for a long time. He finally said to them, "Well, we're not very proud of this, are we?" He had them dig it up and start over again.

President Taylor dedicated the Logan Temple, started weekly priesthood meetings, and instructed Church leaders to begin holding stake conferences. He continued using his wonderful writing talent to teach others the gospel by writing articles for newspapers, books, and pamphlets.

When President Taylor was seventy-eight years old, his health began to fail, and he went to live at the home of a friend in Kaysville, Utah. He died there on July 25, 1887. His son, Frederick W. Taylor said:

> He was one of the great spirits of this world, spending most of his days in the service of God. When I think of his useful life and noble example I feel like praying that we may follow in his footsteps and prove faithful to ourselves and fellow man. I am sure that his work goes on in the sphere where he is.

John Taylor, about age forty-five. Photograph by Marsena Cannon, 1853.

Wilford Woodruff

A Dangerous Young Man to Be Around

Wilford Woodruff was dangerous to be around. Oh, he wasn't mean or cranky. He didn't have a bad temper. In fact he was a gentle, hard-working boy whose greatest desire was to someday meet a real prophet of God.

But being around him was still dangerous. Wilford had been in more accidents, it seemed, than any person in the state of Connecticut. He got an early start. When he was three, he fell into a huge pot of boiling water. He was immediately pulled out, but he was burned badly. When he was five, Wilford fell down a flight of stairs and broke his arm.

Once he was feeding pumpkins to his father's cattle in a pasture. A large bull was eating too much, Wilford decided, so he took a pumpkin away from him. The bull was so angry that he charged Wilford—who held the pumpkin in his arms and ran down the hill as fast as he could go! With the bull right on his heels, Wilford tripped, fell to the ground, and the pumpkin rolled out of his arms. He was astonished when the bull leaped over him, ran his horns into the pumpkin, and tore it to pieces!

Wilford also broke his leg while playing at his father's sawmill. He was kicked in the stomach by an ox. He fell from the top of a hay wagon, and the load of hay toppled over on him.

Another time a wagon overturned on Wilford and his father, and he once fell out of a tree and landed fifteen feet below flat on his back.

As if those accidents weren't enough, Wilford nearly drowned in the Farmington River, nearly froze to death after falling asleep in a blinding snowstorm, was bitten by a sick dog, and at age seventeen was thrown from a horse—breaking one leg and injuring both ankles. There were many more dangerous and hair-raising experiences, but you get the idea: It was dangerous to be around Wilford Woodruff.

How did he survive so many close calls? How was he able to escape death so many times? Wilford answered that himself:

> It seemed to me at times as though some invisible power were watching my footsteps in search of an opportunity to destroy my life. I therefore ascribe my preservation on earth to the watchcare of a merciful Providence, whose hand has been stretched out to rescue me from death when I was in the presence of the most threatening dangers.

Wilford felt sure his life was being spared for a special reason. He often thought of something he was told by a man called "the Old Prophet Mason." Robert Mason, who lived near the Woodruff family in Farmington, Connecticut, was one of the few people in his day who believed in prophets and apostles. He also believed in revelation—that every person was entitled to have his own revelation from God if he prayed sincerely and was worthy to receive it.

Brother Mason visited Wilford in 1830 and told him about a vision he had received thirty years earlier. He had been praying to know the true religion. The Spirit of the Lord told Brother Mason, "My Church is not organized among men in the generation to which you belong; but in the days of your children it shall be made manifest with all the gifts and the blessings enjoyed by the Saints in past ages." Brother Mason then put his hand on Wilford's shoulder and added: "Wilford, I shall never partake of this fruit in the flesh, but you will. And you, my boy, will become a conspicuous actor in the new kingdom."

Wilford didn't understand at first what Brother Mason was trying to tell him. But he tucked it away in his mind and thought of it frequently as he went about doing the two things he liked most: working and fishing.

Wilford's work mostly took place at the flour mill and saw mill that his family owned in Farmington. Both mills were powered by a large paddle wheel turned by a stream that ran past their farm. Wilford's father, Aphek, and his grandfather, Eldad, were very hard workers, and they saw to it that Wilford wasn't just sitting around whittling sticks. Wilford often worked eighteen hours a day.

But when his work was completed, Wilford made a beeline for the stream where he and his brother Azmon loved to fish. The two of them were known as the best fishermen in the area. Wilford was born March 1, 1807, near the banks of this stream, which was full of trout, and some people joked that he began fishing the very next day. He was one of the first in the area to learn how to make artificial flies out of birds' feathers with a hook concealed in each. The fish liked them so well he once caught two fish on one hook!

Wilford discovered an island in the middle of the stream by their farm and claimed it as his own private getaway—a place to which he often went to be alone. When he escaped to this island and lay on his back looking up at the clouds, his thoughts frequently turned to his Heavenly Father. Wilford spent hours, surrounded by wildflowers, praying that he might understand the scriptures he read each day. He wanted to know how he should live. With so many different churches and religions in the area, he wanted to know God's will.

Wilford, unfortunately, had no memory of his mother, Beulah Thompson Woodruff. She died when Wilford was just fifteen months old. She was only twenty-eight when she died of "spotted fever." Within a short time, Wilford's father married Azubah Hart, and she lovingly raised Wilford and his two older brothers, Azmon and Thompson.

In 1833, when Wilford was twenty-six and old enough to be on his own, he decided to move near Richland, New York, where he and Azmon bought a farm. When they weren't farming, they were (of course) fishing. One morning they caught five hundred salmon!

It was there in New York, in late December, that Wilford's life changed in an unexpected way. Azmon's wife, Elizabeth, answered a knock on the door of their home and found two Mormon missionaries standing on the front step. Wilford and Azmon weren't home, so the two elders told Elizabeth to tell the brothers that the missionaries would be preaching at a nearby school house that evening. They would love to have the Woodruffs come and listen to their message about a newly restored church and gospel.

When Wilford arrived home and heard about the missionaries, he remembered Brother Mason's prophecy that he would be a "conspicuous actor in the *new kingdom*." Without waiting for supper, Wilford raced out to his horse and galloped to the schoolhouse! When he arrived, the room was already packed with people. But Wilford eased his way through the crowd and finally got a seat at a writing desk at the very front. He wanted to see and hear everything.

What Wilford saw and heard that night filled his soul with the Spirit of God. "I felt that I had just heard the first true gospel

Wilford Woodruff, age forty-five. Engraver unknown, 1852.

sermon in my life,'' he later said. It was exactly what Wilford had been looking for: prophets, apostles, revelation, spiritual gifts. These were things Wilford knew from studying the Bible, and he knew they were important. He was so excited that he jumped to his feet at the end of the sermon, turned to the crowd, and said, "Friends and neighbors, I feel to tell you not to oppose these men. They are true servants of God. They have preached to us the pure gospel of Jesus Christ. I witness to you it is true!"

Two days later, on December 31, Wilford and Azmon were baptized at a nearby lake. Knowing Wilford, however, you may have guessed that he had an accident or two on his way to the baptism. While getting ready for the ride, his horse suddenly kicked the hat right off Wilford's head. Two inches lower and the hoof probably would have killed the future Prophet. Just ten minutes later, while driving this same horse and another hitched to a sled, several loose boards on the floor of the sled gave way, and Wilford suddenly fell to the ground. With Wilford holding onto the harnesses with all his might, the two frightened horses raced downhill, dragging him along. Luckily, the ground was slick with snow, and he stopped the horses without serious injury.

When Wilford finally got to the lake, the ground at the lake's edge was covered with three feet of snow. Chunks of ice were floating in the water. Nevertheless, Wilford eagerly stepped into the water, was baptized by immersion, and came up filled with joy and excitement. He didn't care that the water was icy cold. All he could think about was having found the Lord's church. Wilford made a promise to the Lord that day to do anything, go anywhere, and sacrifice everything, if need be, for his Heavenly Father.

Wilford Woodruff kept that promise. In fact, Wilford was so loyal and dependable that he was called "Wilford the Faithful."

After his baptism, Wilford's youthful dream of meeting a true prophet of God came true. He rode on horseback to Kirtland, Ohio, and there met the Prophet Joseph Smith. Joseph invited Wilford to stay at his home. While there, he helped Joseph tan a wolf-skin to use on his wagon seat. He also met Brigham

Young and helped him put a good wooden handle on a butcher knife. He learned that these spiritual, loving men were also hard workers.

With Wilford's strong testimony of the gospel came a desire to become a missionary. He wanted to preach. Wilford went into the woods and prayed that he might be able to go on a mission for the Church. He did not have to wait long. Later that same day, a fellow Church member, Elias Higbee, met him on a road and said that the Lord had revealed to him that Brother Wilford Woodruff should be called on a mission. Wilford smiled and said, "I'm ready." He was given a companion, several copies of the Book of Mormon (which he carried in a small traveling bag strapped on his back), and together he and his companion started out. By the end of his mission, Wilford had walked hundreds of miles through Arkansas, Tennessee, and Kentucky.

It was hard work. They encountered bears, were chased by wolves, and waded through swamps up to their waists in mud and water. They were hungry most of the time, too. Some people were kind and fed them a meal or two. Others slammed doors in their faces and turned them away hungry. But they grew spiritually and baptized many people.

Wilford Woodruff became, in fact, one of the greatest missionaries in the Church. After his marriage to Phoebe Carter, when he was thirty years old, he served another mission — this time to the Fox Islands off the coast of Maine. Two years later, when Wilford was thirty-two, he was ordained an apostle. He then served two missions in England, the second one as president of the mission. While in England, Wilford was responsible for baptizing over eighteen hundred people. Two hundred of the people he baptized had been ministers for other churches.

Some people, however, were angry that the Mormon missionaries were so successful. They were upset because they felt

that the elders were taking too many members away from the
other churches and were splitting up families. Because of such
ill feelings, Wilford had to baptize some of the converts late at
night. Once, when he baptized a family at midnight, a mob
gathered and began throwing stones from the edge of the pond.
One large rock hit Wilford on the head and almost knocked him
down, but he completed the baptism.

During this difficult time, the Lord helped Wilford in many
ways. Sacred experiences seemed even more plentiful than dangerous accidents. Heavenly messengers visited Wilford. One
night, when he felt that Satan was trying to discourage him, he
prayed for help. Three personages dressed in white appeared and
"healed him." He immediately felt at peace.

Another time, while traveling at night on horseback through
a heavy rainstorm, he and his companions were suddenly surrounded by a bright beam of light. It saved them from taking a
dangerous trail and lit the way to a friendly house nearby.

Wilford faithfully recorded all these experiences in his journal—which he wrote in every day for sixty-three years! Wilford
wrote not only about the most important events of his life, but
also he described his everyday activities: buying oranges from a
farmer in London, suffering from sea sickness while crossing
the ocean, digging for clams, or walking on sore feet. He wrote
down many of Joseph Smith's sermons, which are precious to
the Church today. He often decorated the journal pages with
elaborate drawings and illustrations. Wilford's journals are now
very valuable. They tell us a great deal about the history of the
Church.

In 1847 Wilford and his family crossed the plains with the
first pioneer company and entered the Salt Lake Valley alongside
Brigham Young. He continued to serve as an apostle and missionary and was Church historian for more than thirty years.

The third Book of Wilford for 1837

O Lord I ask thee in the name of Jesus Christ thy Son, to look upon thy servant Willford, Who now occupies a place in Kirtland, this first stake of Zion, which thou hast appointed in this last Dispensation, & fulness of times for the gathering of thy Saints. O God of Israel, inspire the heart & Pen of thy Servant at this time, & hear & answer the Petition which he will put up unto thee at this time, & remember the Covenant which thy servant Willford will make with thee at this time, O mighty God of Jacob. O Lord thou hast spared my life, to behold the Commencem of 1837. May my life, health, & strength be precious in thy Sight, throu' the year. Wilt thou save me by thy grace from all sin, & the Powers of temptation, which try the souls of men. Wilt thou give me favor during this year, with God & the Saints. Wilt thou bless me while in School, & in meeting with the quorum of the Seventies, & while attending all other meetings in Kirtland for Divine worship. O Lord if it be thy will give me the privilege of recording in this years Journal great blessings, Pronounced upon my head from mine annointing & from under the hands of the Patriarch JOSEPH. & an account of Great visions, & the opening of the heavens, & the reve-lation of JESUS CHRIST unto me that I may be a special witness of Thee. O Lord. & may I also have the administering of Holy angels, that I may be taught of the Eternal things of the Priesthood. If I am called to Preach thy word this year, may I be bless with souls for my hire. if I visit my Kinsman, wilt thou make me an instrument, of bringing them into thy Celestial Kingdom. & I Covenant with Thee, Heavenly FATHER, to go & come at thy bidding, I ask the above blessings, through the Priesthood, in the name of **JESUS CHRIST AMEN.**

Page from Wilford Woodruff's journal recording a prayer to begin the year 1837. He was twenty-nine years old at the time. Photographer unknown.

He was also a government and business leader and joined scientific, medical, and gardening societies.

Wilford had a large family. He lived the principle of plural marriage and had five wives and thirty-three children. One of the things Wilford enjoyed doing with his family was working outdoors. Even as an elderly man, he could be seen outside hoeing and planting on his farm alongside his grandchildren.

On one occasion, when he was ninety years old, Wilford was disturbed that one of his grandchildren finished hoeing a patch of vegetables just a little before he did. Wilford wiped his brow and said, "I'm getting old. That's the first time in my life that one of my grandchildren has ever outdone me in hoeing."

Wilford won many ribbons for his farm projects at the territorial fairs. He won first prizes for best fenced and cultivated farm of not less than twenty acres, best acre of sugar cane, best three acres of squash, best six acres of sugar beets, best bush beans, best three cantaloupes, best apples, and best grapes. One year he produced one thousand five hundred gallons of syrup from his three acres of sugar cane. That would cover a lot of Saturday morning flapjacks!

In 1877, Wilford had a marvelous vision while in the St. George Temple. He was visited by the signers of the Declaration of Independence. They told him they wanted to have their temple work done for them. Wilford was then baptized for more than a hundred people, including Thomas Jefferson, Benjamin Franklin, Christopher Columbus, and Charles Louis Bonaparte.

After serving as an apostle for fifty years, Wilford Woodruff became the fourth president of the Church in 1889. He was eighty-three years old. At this age, most other people were "taking it easy." President Woodruff, however, was just beginning one of the busiest times of his life. He knew it was going to be

The First Presidency on Wilford Woodruff's eighty-seventh birthday. Wilford Woodruff is standing. George Q. Cannon, first counselor, is to left; Joseph F. Smith, second counselor, is to the right. Photograph by C. R. Savage, 1894.

The laying of the capstone of the Salt Lake Temple. Photograph by C. R. Savage, April 1892.

a great challenge. After being sustained as prophet of the Church, he said to the Saints:

> This is a high and responsible position for any man to occupy and a position that needs great wisdom. God has certainly chosen the weak things of this world to perform [His] work on the earth. May thy servant Wilford be prepared for whatever is required at his hands by the God of Heaven.

President Woodruff did many important things while serving

as prophet: he dedicated the Salt Lake Temple, he changed fast day from the first Thursday of each month to the first Sunday of each month, Utah became a state while he was president, and he received "The Manifesto," the revelation in which Heavenly Father told him that the members of the Church should no longer live the law of plural marriage.

Wilford's love of fishing continued throughout his life. When he returned from one of his missions to England, he proudly brought home a new kind of fishing pole that had just been invented: a fly rod. While crossing the plains with Brigham Young, he fished the streams all the way along, providing dinner many times for some of his group. Even after becoming president of the Church, Wilford was often seen out in a boat on a stream or lake, quietly fishing.

President Wilford Woodruff died September 2, 1898, at the age of ninety-two, in San Francisco, California, where he had gone for health reasons. He had kept his promise to go anywhere, do anything, and sacrifice whatever was necessary for the gospel. To the end he remained: "Wilford the Faithful."

Lorenzo Snow

Soldier for the Lord

Lorenzo Snow dreamed of being a soldier. Both of his grand-fathers had served in the American Revolutionary War, and he loved hearing again and again the exciting stories of danger in their service to their country. Lorenzo often sat at the knee of his Grandfather Snow, listening to his military adventures. He remembered vividly one of his Grandfather's most hair-raising experiences:

> While fighting for the freedom of our country, [Grand-father Snow] was taken prisoner by the British troops, and confined in a dreary cell. He was so scantily fed that when his fellow-prisoner by his side died from exhaustion, Grand-father reported him to the jailor as sick in bed, in order to obtain the amount of food for both—keeping him covered in their blankets as long as he dared to remain with a de-caying body!

Such stories horrified some of the other grandchildren, but they made Lorenzo tingle with excitement. He even talked his sister Eliza into sewing a military uniform for him. He called it his "freedom suit." When she completed it and Lorenzo tried it on, they both agreed it was "beautiful and magnificent."

Lorenzo felt proud and imagined himself out on the battlefield leading his troops to victory.

Lorenzo would become a soldier all right, but a very different kind of soldier than the one of his boyhood dreams. He would join the "Lord's army" and be sent forth to countries all over the world to preach the gospel. Lorenzo would celebrate the victory of bringing many wonderful people into the Lord's church. The weapons would not be guns or swords but scripture and truth. But never fear—the danger and excitement would still be there.

Lorenzo was born April 3, 1814, on a farm in Mantua, Portage County, Ohio. He had four older sisters and two younger brothers. His parents, Oliver and Rosetta Pettibone Snow, had met and married in Massachusetts before moving to Ohio to help settle a new area. Oliver was a rugged and hard-working man who served as a county commissioner and a justice of the peace. If anyone broke the law or got into a quarrel that couldn't be settled, Oliver Snow was the man to see.

The Snow family belonged to the Baptist Church, but they welcomed people of all religions to their home. Their farm was some distance from town, and they frequently offered a warm place to sleep and breakfast to any traveler who became lost or stranded in a winter snowstorm.

One such traveler stopped at their home and changed their lives forever. During the winter of 1831–32, a tall, twenty-six-year-old man with sandy-colored hair named Joseph Smith, Jr., knocked on their door.

The Snow family had heard of Joseph Smith two years earlier and were interested in hearing from this man who called himself a "prophet." Eliza was especially fascinated with Joseph. "I scrutinized his face as closely as I could without attracting his attention," she later wrote, "and decided that his was an honest face."

Lorenzo listened with interest, but his mind was distracted by other things. At least for now, he was thinking more about school. Lorenzo had always wanted to be a military officer, and for that he needed a college education. So, when he was twenty-one years old, he saddled his horse and began the twenty-five-mile ride east to Oberlin College. But Lorenzo met a man along the way who would bring him to the restored gospel.

Elder David W. Patten, an apostle of The Church of Jesus Christ of Latter-day Saints, was returning home on horseback from a mission to Canada when he and Lorenzo crossed paths. Elder Patten was more than happy to tell young Lorenzo about the gospel as they rode along together. Lorenzo was impressed with his strong testimony. He wrote:

> I felt pricked in my heart. The last thing [Elder Patten] said to me after bearing his testimony was that I should go to the Lord before retiring at night and ask him for myself [if the gospel is true]. This I did. It was the turning point of my life.

During his year at college, Lorenzo used his spare time to study "Mormonism" inside and out. He went to Kirtland, Ohio, and listened to the Prophet Joseph Smith speak several times. "As I looked upon him and listened," Lorenzo wrote, "I thought to myself that a man bearing such a wonderful testimony as he did and having such a countenance as he possessed could hardly be a false prophet."

Lorenzo was baptized in June, 1836. Soon afterward, he went into a wooded area to pray:

> I had no sooner opened my lips in an effort to pray, than

I heard a sound, just above my head, like the rustling of silken robes and immediately the Spirit of God descended upon me, completely enveloping my whole person, filling me, from the crown of my head to the soles of my feet, and O, the joy and happiness I felt. . . . I then received a perfect knowledge that God lives, that Jesus Christ is the son of God, of the restoration of the holy Priesthood, and the fullness of the Gospel.

It was one of the most spiritual experiences of Lorenzo's life. After having such a thrilling witness, he was fully ready to become a "soldier" for the Lord's church.

Lorenzo immediately requested permission to go on a mission. Not only was this request granted, but he would eventually go on six missions for the Church. He taught the gospel in his boyhood state of Ohio, as well as Missouri, Kentucky, Illinois, the southern United States, Italy, Malta, Switzerland, Holland, Hawaii, and Great Britain, where he gave Queen Victoria and her husband, Prince Albert, a copy of the Book of Mormon.

While serving in Ohio, Lorenzo had a dream one night in which he saw an angry mob attacking him in a schoolhouse. The next day, two well-dressed men came to him and asked him to come to a schoolhouse where a crowd was waiting to hear his message. Remembering the dream, Lorenzo refused to come. They tried harder to get him to come, but Lorenzo would not. They finally left, shouting angry words at him. Lorenzo later learned that a mob had been waiting for him at the school. They weren't waiting to hear him preach, however. They were waiting to attack him.

Another time, in Kentucky, Lorenzo was warming himself by a fire at the end of a meeting. A rough character standing beside him, who was part of a gang waiting to attack him, accidentally bumped against Lorenzo and felt his scriptures in a jacket pocket. (The scriptures were a gift from Joseph Smith, Sr.) The man thought the object in Lorenzo's jacket was a gun, and he immediately left without causing a fight.

At the end of his mission in Kentucky, Lorenzo walked five hundred miles back to Ohio in the winter. When he arrived in Ohio at the home of relatives, Lorenzo was so thin and exhausted that they didn't even recognize him at first and refused to let him in their home.

In 1840, by inspiration from the Holy Ghost, Lorenzo was able to put into simple words a new principle, which would become a very important part of the restored gospel. Lorenzo expressed the principle this way: "As man now is, God once was. As God now is, man may become." When Lorenzo talked to the Prophet Joseph Smith about this principle, Joseph told him it was "true doctrine and a revelation from God."

Two of Lorenzo's best friends (believe it or not) were his sisters, Leonora and Eliza. They also joined the Church, and the three of them gave each other much love and support while the Church suffered through difficult times of persecution. Once while they were traveling together in a wagon from Kirtland to Far West, Missouri, Lorenzo got a terrible headache that lasted for days. His sister Eliza kindly held his head in her hands and on her lap during the journey to cushion it from the wagon's rough movements.

In 1846, the Saints were driven out of Nauvoo, Illinois, and a group of pioneers lived for a short time in Pisgah, Iowa. President Brigham Young asked Lorenzo to preside over this group for several months. Lorenzo was an energetic leader. He tried to keep everybody happy and content by organizing activities and gatherings. The people frequently came to Lorenzo's home, a fifteen-by-thirty-foot log cabin with a dirt floor, lit by candles in scooped-out turnips. Their evenings were spent in dancing,

Eliza Roxey Snow, elder sister of Lorenzo Snow. Photograph by C. W. Carter.

singing, trading riddles, giving speeches, telling stories, and (of course) having refreshments. Who knows, maybe they had the turnips for the refreshments.

The following spring in 1848, Lorenzo was called by Brigham Young to lead a large group of pioneers to the Salt Lake Valley.

His company included 321 people, 99 wagons, 20 horses, 3 mules, 388 oxen, 188 cows, 38 loose cattle, 139 sheep, 25 pigs, 159 chickens. They also had 10 cats, 26 dogs, and 2 doves.

Soon after his company's safe arrival in the Salt Lake Valley on September 22, 1848, Lorenzo was called to the Council of the Twelve Apostles. He was surprised to receive such an important calling, but he promised to "be inspired by the Holy Ghost" and to help President Brigham Young by doing whatever he was asked to do.

As an apostle, Lorenzo Snow led a very busy life. He served as a counselor in the First Presidency to President Brigham Young, he served in the territorial legislature for thirty years, and he went on short missions for the Church. One of Lorenzo's most enjoyable missions was to the Holy Land to see where the Savior had lived while on the earth.

While serving a mission to Hawaii, Lorenzo nearly drowned in a terrifying accident at sea. While traveling between two islands, Lorenzo was riding in a small boat with several others when they were suddenly caught in a storm. The strong winds sent mountainous waves racing toward their boat "swifter than a race horse." When one especially big wave came by, their boat flipped over, tossing the men in all directions.

When other members of the group finally came up from the churning water, coughing and gasping for air, Lorenzo was nowhere in sight. They searched frantically for several minutes, unable to find him. Then, one of the Hawaiian natives felt Lorenzo's body beneath the water and pulled him up. Lorenzo was not breathing and appeared to be dead.

They hurried Lorenzo to shore, where the Elders administered to him, pleading with Heavenly Father "to spare his life that he might return to his family and home." Working quickly, they placed Lorenzo's body over an empty barrel and rolled him

Lorenzo Snow, age thirty-eight. Engraving by Fredrick Piercy, 1852.

back and forth until the water came out of his lungs . A small crowd had gathered on shore to watch their efforts. They thought that any help was useless — he was already dead.

Then, the elders felt inspired to give him mouth-to-mouth resuscitation, a technique rarely used at that time. Soon they noticed a slight wink in Lorenzo's eyes, and he began to respond. Lorenzo was alive! Nearly an hour had passed since their boat had capsized, but he was going to be all right.

Lorenzo was glad to get home safe and sound after the near-drowning. He had a large family to take care of. Lorenzo Snow had nine wives over a period of many years and forty-one children. He went to great effort to build homes that would be happy places for his children. In one of their houses, Lorenzo added a large room with a stage that the children used as a small theater. They loved putting on plays for their friends and neighbors.

Lorenzo Snow had been living in the Salt Lake Valley only five years when President Young gave him a challenging new assignment: to become the leader of a new community in Box Elder County, Utah, sixty miles north of Salt Lake City. The settlement would later be known as Brigham City. Some settlers were already living in the area, but they needed an energetic leader to organize things and inspire them to work harder.

When Lorenzo first arrived in the settlement with fifty new families, he was discouraged to see the farms and buildings in such poor condition. He complained, "Even the meetinghouse with its dirt floor and earth roof was more fit to be visited by bed bugs than the Saints."

Lorenzo worked hard to improve life in Brigham City. He started a public school system, a theatre company, and businesses of all kinds. Hammering could be heard all day long, and new buildings went up everywhere. During the day a visitor could see settlers making everything from saddles, shoes, and hats to brooms, wagons, cheese, butter, and furniture. Some evenings, the Saints flocked to the social hall to dance to the accompaniment of a violin, cornet, or guitar. They fasted each month to raise money for the poor people and held outdoor band concerts and grand parades on special occasions. Under the leadership of Lorenzo Snow, Brigham City soon became a busy, happy community.

When Lorenzo Snow received his patriarchal blessing from Joseph Smith, Sr., he was promised:

> Thou hast a great work to perform in thy day and generation. Thou shalt have faith even like that of the brother of Jared. There shall not be a mightier man on earth than thou. If expedient *the dead shall rise* and come forth at thy bidding.

This blessing came true for Lorenzo Snow. While conducting a church conference, he was handed a note that said a young girl who lived nearby had died. The note asked him if he would help make arrangements for her funeral. Elder Snow immediately excused himself from the meeting and went to the girl's home where her family was mourning her death.

After praying to the Lord for help, Elder Snow asked the father of the family if he had any consecrated oil in the house. The father was surprised to hear him ask for this since his daughter had already died, but he got Elder Snow the oil. Lorenzo then anointed the girl and blessed her to come back to life and be healed because she had not finished her work here on the earth. Elder Snow then told the parents not to feel sad anymore. Their daughter would soon come back to life.

Within an hour the daughter opened her eyes, sat up in bed, and asked, "Where is he? Where is he?" Her mother said, "Where is who?" The daughter replied, "Where is Brother Snow? He called me back to this earth." Ella Jensen, the girl who was healed, lived a long life and became the mother of eight children.

Lorenzo Snow served five years beginning in 1893 as the first president of the Salt Lake Temple. In fact, he was in that temple when he had his greatest and most humbling spiritual experience. He told his granddaughter Allie Young Pond exactly what happened, and she described it this way:

> One evening while I was visiting Grandpa Snow in his room in the Salt Lake Temple, I remained until the door-keepers had gone and the night-watchmen had not yet come in. Grandpa said he would take me to the main front entrance and let me out that way. He got his bunch of keys from his dresser. After we left his room and while we were still in the large corridor leading into the celestial room, I was walking several steps ahead of grandpa when he stopped me and said: "Wait a moment, Allie, I want to tell you something. It was right here that the Lord Jesus Christ appeared to me at the time of the death of President Woodruff. He instructed me to go right ahead and reorganize the First Presidency of the Church at once and not wait as had been done after the death of the previous presidents. I was to succeed President Woodruff" [as president of the Church].
>
> Then grandpa came a step nearer and held out his left hand and said: "He stood right here, about three feet above the floor. It looked as though He stood on a plate of solid Gold."
>
> Grandpa told me what a glorious personage the Savior is and described His hands, feet, countenance and beautiful white robes, all of which were of such a glory of whiteness and brightness that he could hardly gaze upon Him.
>
> Then he came another step nearer and put his right hand on my head and said: "Now granddaughter, I want you to remember that this is the testimony of your grandfather, that he told you with his own lips that he actually saw the Savior, here in the Temple, and talked with Him face to face."

Lorenzo Snow was eighty-four years old when he became

*First Presidency and the Quorum of the Twelve Apostles, September
1898. President Lorenzo Snow is seated, third from left. George Q.
Cannon, first counselor, is seated, third from right; Joseph F. Smith,
second from right. Heber J. Grant, a future president of the Church,
is standing, third from right. Photographer unknown.*

president of the Church in 1898. In spite of his age, President
Snow made great and lasting contributions to the Church as its
fifth prophet, seer, and revelator.

At this time the Church owed a great deal of money to many
businesses and banks and was struggling to pay its bills. Many
thought the Church would fail and disappear because of its

Lorenzo Snow, about age seventy-eight. Photograph by C. W. Carter, ca. 1892.

money problems. Then, while traveling to St. George, Utah, during a severe drought, President Snow felt inspired by the Holy Ghost to tell the Saints at a special conference that they had been "neglecting the law of tithing." If they would begin from that day forth to pay a full tithing, he promised them the rains would come and they would "become a prosperous people."

On his way back to Salt Lake City from St. George, President Snow stopped along the way at sixteen small Utah communities and gave them the same message.

The Saints took his counsel to heart and the amount of tithing paid to the Church grew in leaps and bounds over the next months. Their obedience to this principle helped the Church solve its financial problems. And, as a result of the Saints' obedience, the rains came as President Snow had promised they would.

Lorenzo Snow served as president of the Church for three years and died October 10, 1901, at the age of eighty-seven. The children of the Church paid special tribute to him at his funeral. As the procession moved along the streets of Salt Lake City, over one thousand Primary-aged children who were dressed in their Sunday best lined the streets and formed an "honor guard" for the Lord's soldier. They threw flowers in the path of the procession as it moved toward the Tabernacle. After the services, President Snow was buried in Brigham City, Utah.

A minister once said of President Lorenzo Snow: "His spirit is as gentle as a child. You are introduced to him and you are pleased with him. You converse with him and you like him. You visit with him long and you love him!"

Lorenzo Snow, about age eighty-six. Photograph by C. R. Savage, ca. 1900.

Joseph F. Smith

An Orphan at the Age of Thirteen

It was late at night, and five-year-old Joseph F. Smith was lying in bed. But his eyes were wide open, and he was having trouble getting to sleep. It had rained earlier in the day and then had grown hot and muggy.

Although still very young, Joseph F. was old enough to understand that his father, Hyrum Smith, was in great danger. Three days earlier, Hyrum had left their home in Nauvoo, Illinois, with his younger brother, the Prophet Joseph Smith. They went to a nearby town, Carthage, to answer charges made by people who accused them of wrong-doing. Hyrum and Joseph knew they were in danger because of the destruction of the *Nauvoo Expositor* press, a paper that printed vicious lies about them and the Church. But they were willing to go and clear up any misunderstandings.

Now, as Joseph F. lay awake, he remembered saying goodbye to his father. He had been standing out by the road in front of their home. Hyrum rode up to him on horseback and said, "Son, we have been ordered to go to Carthage to meet with the governor." Then leaning forward from his saddle, he picked Joseph F. up. "I must leave you now," he said tenderly. "Be a brave boy and help your dear mother all you can." He kissed his young son, gave him a warm hug, and carefully set him back down on the ground.

Hyrum rode away with several other men. Young Joseph F. remembered wondering if he would ever see his father alive again. He knew that many people wanted to see the Church and its leaders destroyed.

Suddenly, Joseph F. sat up in bed as he heard someone knocking loudly on the window downstairs. He heard the words that broke his heart. A man outside the window called out in a trembling voice, "Sister Smith, Sister Smith, we bring you sad news. Your husband has been killed."

Joseph F.'s father, Hyrum, and the Prophet Joseph had been shot by a mob as they were being held at Carthage Jail. The date was June 27, 1844, and Hyrum was forty-four years old. Young Joseph F. would remember it as the saddest day of his life.

Heartbroken and frightened, little Joseph F. lay awake the rest of the night listening to the sobbing of his mother. Now as never before, his life would center around her, his faithful, courageous mother, Mary Fielding Smith.

Hyrum Smith had married Mary Fielding on December 24, 1837, after his first wife, Jerusha, died while giving birth to their fifth child. Mary accepted the responsibility of caring for Hyrum's children, believing it was the will of the Lord.

Joseph F. was born at a time when the Smith family was suffering its greatest trials. Joseph F. (whose full name was Joseph Fielding Smith) was born November 13, 1838, in Far West, Missouri. At the time of his birth, his father had been unfairly put in jail, tried for a variety of crimes, and even sentenced to death. Only the courage of an officer who refused to carry out the order to execute him saved Hyrum's life.

One night, while Hyrum was in prison, several angry men

broke into the Smith home, pushing the women and children into a corner of the main room. They began ransacking the house, looking for Hyrum's papers and other valuables. Without knowing it, they threw a mattress on top of little baby Joseph F., who lay sleeping on a nearby bed. The baby was discovered soon after the men rode away. Little Joseph F. could easily have suffocated, but the life of the future prophet was saved.

When Joseph F. was just two months old, he was laid in a wagon bed alongside his mother for a special trip. Together with his Aunt Mercy Fielding Thompson, his cousin Mary Jane, and his Aunt Emma Smith, they traveled forty miles on a rough and bumpy road to visit Hyrum and Joseph in Liberty Jail. The cell where the prisoners were held was crowded and filthy. But even in such a sorry place, Hyrum rejoiced to see for the first time his infant son.

Joseph F.'s father was a handsome man. Over six feet tall, dark and broad-shouldered, Hyrum was a faithful companion to his brother, the Prophet Joseph. He helped Joseph organize the Church in 1830, served as the Church patriarch, and was one of the eight witnesses who saw and held the gold plates from which Joseph Smith translated the Book of Mormon.

Perhaps some evenings Hyrum sat Joseph F. on his knee in front of the fireplace and told him about the golden plates. He may have told of the unusual writing on the plates, which could be translated only with the help of God. Hyrum surely must have described how very heavy they were—about sixty pounds, the weight of a ten-year-old-child.

After the death of Hyrum and Joseph, President Brigham Young told the Saints that they must leave Nauvoo if they were to find peace. Their destination would be a place they believed God had prepared for them. There they hoped to worship God without fear of persecution.

Hyrum Smith, father of Joseph F. Smith. Engraving by Fredrick Piercy.

Joseph F., at the age of seven, drove their ox team two hundred miles to Winter Quarters, a temporary stopping place on the west bank of the Missouri River. His five-year-old sister, Martha Ann, often sat by him on the driver's seat. Mary, her children, and stepchildren lived there a year and a half while they prepared for the journey west.

As they traveled, Joseph F. cared for the animals, chopped wood for their cooking fires, and hauled water from nearby streams. He was having to do the work of a man while still a young boy.

In the spring of 1848, Mary Fielding Smith's little caravan joined the rest of a wagon train of other faithful Latter-day Saints and began the thousand-mile journey west to the Salt Lake Valley. In addition to her children and stepchildren, Mary's group included her widowed sister Mercy Thompson and her brother Joseph Fielding. As they began their long journey, the reins of one of Mary's four wagons were in the firm grip of her nine-year-old son, Joseph F. By now Joseph was an excellent driver. He was experienced in yoking and unyoking the oxen and carefully guided the animals over many dangerous trails from his perch on the driver's seat.

As the wagon train moved along, it must have been a sight to behold. One pioneer described the scene as "a train of white wagon sheets many miles in length, looking like an immense serpent dragging his slow lengths along."

During the next three months, Joseph F. would gain an even greater appreciation of his mother's great faith in the Lord. They woke up one morning to find two of their finest oxen missing. Several men looked for a long time without finding the animals. After they gave up, Joseph F. returned to the camp to find his mother on her knees praying for the Lord's help. "Please lead us to the oxen that we might continue our journey in safety," he heard her plead.

As soon as she finished her prayer, she stood up. Joseph F. saw his mother walk straight to a nearby river. One of the men shouted that she was going the wrong way — they had been seen

Pioneer wagon train moves through Echo Canyon, Utah, in the early 1860s. Photograph by C. W. Carter.

going the other direction! But Mary motioned for Joseph F. to come quickly. There were the oxen, caught in a clump of willows down in a ravine. They were soon hitched to the wagon and on their way again.

In spite of many such difficulties, the journey across the plains must have seemed exciting to Joseph F. With hundreds of families making the trip, there was always something going on. He saw his first herd of buffalo and enjoyed swimming in watering holes near camp. To lift his spirits for the next day's journey, he joined with the others in singing songs at night around the campfire. "Come, Come Ye Saints" was always a favorite. One day each week was also a "rest day." Worship services were held, after which Joseph F. and his friends would pick gooseberries, hike over to an abandoned Indian village, or throw lumps of dirt at garfish in the streams.

The wagon trains were well organized, each with a captain to take charge. Men were assigned each night to stand guard, and they were kept company by the night's bats and croaking frogs. A few incidents with Indians put the guards on special alert. Woe to the guard who fell asleep during his watch!

And there were rules to follow: Do not yell or make any noise at night, so as not to disturb the others; tie up all your hogs and dogs, remember your evening prayers, and be in bed by 9 P.M. And *please,* be kind to your animals.

Joseph F. was especially kind to his animals and felt sorry for the oxen having to pull such heavy loads day after day. Later in his life, he told his own children:

> My team leaders' names were Thom and Joe—we raised them from calves and they were both white. Thom was trim built, active, young and more intelligent than many a man. Many times while traveling sandy or rough roads, [on] long, thirsty drives, my oxen [were] lowing with the heat and fatigue. I would put my arms around Thom's neck, and cry bitter tears! That was all I could do. Thom was my favorite and best and most willing and obedient servant and friend. He was choice!

With the Lord's constant help, the Smiths finally arrived in the Salt Lake Valley on September 23, 1848. But their troubles were far from over. They had to live the first winter in their covered wagon until they were able to build a small adobe home the following spring on Mill Creek.

They were very poor—everyone was. But Mary taught Joseph F. an important lesson by insisting they pay their tithing first, before they used any of the produce from their garden. "The Lord's share must be the best pick of the crop," she would tell Joseph F. as she instructed him to pick out the best potatoes to take to the tithing office.

Joseph F. was still missing his father, Hyrum, when he experienced yet another great sorrow. His mother's health was very bad, and she died just four years after their arrival in the Salt Lake Valley. When his father was killed, Joseph F. was five years old. Now when his mother died, he was thirteen. He was still so young! How would he survive? Who would take care of him? He felt alone and frightened.

But the Lord had plans for Joseph F. Smith. A year and a half later, the Lord called Joseph F. on a mission to preach the gospel to the people of the Hawaiian Islands. He was fifteen years old, an unusually young age for a missionary. To comfort him, the Lord blessed him with a beautiful dream. He dreamed that, when his life was over, his beloved mother and father, the Prophet Joseph Smith, and President Brigham Young met him in heaven. They put their arms around him, and he could feel how much they loved him. It made him feel so peaceful inside.

Joseph F. later said, "When I awoke that morning, I was a man. There was not anything in the world that I feared. I promised myself that I would so live that both Mother and Father would be proud of me." Now he had the courage to do whatever the Lord would ask of him.

There was a great work for him yet to do. The mission president, Francis Hammond, gave Joseph F. a blessing, promising him he would become "a mighty man" and that "the spirit of his father Hyrum, the martyr, would rest upon him."

Joseph F. learned the Hawaiian language quickly and became an excellent missionary. He was very poor, however, since he had no family to send him money. Joseph F. ate poi, sweet potatoes, and chili peppers, which the Hawaiian people shared

Joseph F. Smith, about age nineteen.
Photographer unknown, ca. 1857

Joseph F. Smith in his early twenties.
Photographer unknown.

with him. He often went for several days without anything to eat.

After three years in Hawaii, Joseph F. returned home. One morning during his adventurous trip back to Salt Lake City, he and several other companions were sitting around a campfire fixing breakfast. A group of rough Mormon-haters rode up on horses, cursing and firing their guns.

The leader jumped off his horse and shouted, "We will kill anyone who is a Mormon!" The other missionaries fled into the woods, but Joseph F. stood his ground. The man shoved a gun in Joseph's face and asked, "Are you a Mormon?" Joseph F.

straightened his shoulders and said, "Yes siree; dyed in the wool; true blue, through and through!"

The man was surprised at his reply. He put the gun away, shook Joseph's hand, and said, "Well, you are the pleasantest man I ever met! I'm glad to see a fellow stand for his convictions." He then jumped back on his horse and rode off with his companions.

For the next sixty-one years, Joseph F. Smith's life was full of service to the church he defended so proudly that morning by the campfire. At age twenty-seven, he was ordained an apostle, and he served as a counselor to four Church presidents: Brigham Young, John Taylor, Wilford Woodruff, and Lorenzo Snow. Joseph F. served four more missions for the Church, in England, Europe, and twice again in Hawaii. He worked as a clerk in the Historian's Office, supervised work in the Endowment House, and served in the Utah legislature.

After President Snow's death in 1901, Joseph F. Smith was sustained as president of the Church. He was sixty-three years old.

Because of the revelation President Lorenzo Snow had received in 1899 concerning tithing, the Church's money problems continued to improve during the years Joseph F. Smith served as president. By 1906, President Smith was able to free the Church completely from the debt they owed to the government and other businesses. Without this being done, the Church could have lost much of its land, church buildings, and even the temples. Rachel Smith, one of his daughters, remembers the exact day this happened:

> Father came home, but no one was there in the house. As I was coming in the side door of the Beehive House, I met him coming down the front stairs. He said to me, "Baby" (he always called us babies), "where is Mother?"

I said, "I don't know." Father asked me several questions for which my answer was "I don't know." Finally Father said, "Well what do you know?" I replied "Not much. I just came from school."

Father said, "I wanted to tell your mother first, but . . . I'll tell you first. Do you see this paper I have in my hand?" I answered yes. "Well, [this note means] the Church is at last out of debt!"

Children all over the world have especially benefited from three important changes President Smith made during his presidency: the Church began publishing the *Children's Friend* magazine (later called the *Friend*) in 1902, the seminary program was started in 1912, and the family home evening program began in 1915.

President Smith thought frequently about his boyhood and returned several times to visit the places he had lived during his early years. While visiting Nauvoo, Illinois, his boyhood home until the Saints were driven out, Joseph F. said, "I recognized it as tho I had lived there all my life. There stood our old barn and brick office as they did years ago. I could pick out nearly every spot that I had known in my childhood."

While in Nauvoo, he visited his aunt, Emma Smith, widow of the Prophet Joseph. As soon as he greeted her, she said, "Why, it is Joseph Fielding! I would have known you anywhere, you look so much like your father Hyrum!" This comment pleased Joseph F., and he considered it a great compliment.

But Joseph F. visited other sites that brought back painful memories. Later in his life, he finally gathered the courage to visit Carthage Jail where his father was murdered. While standing inside the jail, he told his friend, "I despise this place. It harrows up my feelings to come here." He stood silently for a

Joseph F. Smith (center); five of his wives, Mary Schwartz (seated left), Edna Lambson (seated second from left), Julina Lambson (seated third from left), Sarah Richards (seated third from right), Alice Kimball (seated second from right); and their children and grandchildren. Photographer unknown, 1898.

while. Then he turned, walked out of the building, and never returned.

President Smith lived the law of plural marriage and had six wives and forty-eight children (five were adopted). Because he had lost his own parents at such an early age, his family meant everything to him. He once said, "The richest of all my earthly joys is in my precious children." A close friend of the family,

Charles W. Nibley, who was frequently in President Smith's home, wrote:

> I have visited at his home when one of his children was down sick. I have seen him come home from his work at night tired, as he naturally would be, and yet he would walk the floor for hours with that little one in his arms, . . . loving it, encouraging it in every way with such tenderness and such a soul of pity and love as not one [parent] in a thousand would show.

One of his daughters, Marjorie Smith Brown, remembers that, as a little girl, she was very frightened of thunder and lightning:

> One day there was a very bad storm. I was crying and whimpering. Father got up, put his robe on, and came in. He had me put my robe and slippers on; then we walked out on the veranda, attached to the second floor of the Beehive House. He held my hand, and that gave me a feeling of security and strength. Still, when the sky would light up, I would tremble. Father explained to me what lightning meant and what made the noise. Then he said, "See it will bring the rain that will make everything so beautiful. You must not be afraid." From that day to this I have never been frightened of a thunderstorm.

Just a few months before he died, President Smith received a beautiful, magnificent vision. In it, he saw Jesus during the time the Savior's body lay in the tomb for three days following his crucifixion. The Savior was visiting the spirits of those who had already died. President Smith saw Jesus organizing many of the righteous spirits to help preach the gospel to those spirits who needed to be taught. Among the "faithful" who were teaching others were his own father Hyrum and the Prophet Joseph

The First Presidency from 1901–1910. Joseph F. Smith is center. John R. Winder, first counselor, is left; Anthon H. Lund, second counselor, is right. Photographer unknown.

Smith. This vision was later published as Section 138 of the Doctrine and Covenants.

President Joseph F. Smith died on November 19, 1918, just six days after his eightieth birthday. The great flu epidemic was raging in Salt Lake City. To prevent this disease from spreading any further, no public funeral was held. But as his funeral procession passed from the Beehive House to the city cemetery, thousands of people stood mourning along the streets with bowed heads.

Joseph F. Smith had many sorrows in his life—the greatest

of which was losing both of his parents by age thirteen. But he learned a great lesson: he found that if he prayed to and relied on his Heavenly Father for help and comfort, he would be able to accomplish almost anything. And what this orphan boy accomplished in his life under the Lord's direction was remarkable.

Heber J. Grant

Baseball Hero

Twelve-year-old Heber J. Grant shook like a leaf as he looked out into the audience in the Brigham Young Schoolhouse in Salt Lake City. It certainly wasn't the first time he had stood in front of a group to recite a memorized scripture, story, or talk. But this occasion was different. As Heber forced himself to look again at the audience, he saw President Brigham Young himself sitting on the third row. Heber knew he was just about to speak in front of one of the most famous and experienced orators in the whole Territory of Utah!

The situation proved to be almost too much for young Heber. He walked up to the front and proceeded to stumble badly through a memorized recitation of the Word of Wisdom—a presentation he had given perfectly dozens of times before other groups. At one point he completely stopped his reading, unable to remember the next few lines.

Finally Heber started again from the beginning—this time getting through it with little problem. He took his seat, feeling very disappointed at his performance. But President Young came up to him after the meeting, put his arm around Heber's shoulder, and praised him for the courage he had shown by not quitting. Heber remembered the president saying, "You demonstrated a true spirit of determination to accomplish the task given to you. Your father would have been very proud.''

Heber smiled at the thought of making his father proud. Heber Jeddy Grant was born in Salt Lake City on November 22, 1856. Rachel Ivins Grant, his mother, was still in bed recovering from his birth when she was brought the sad news that Jedediah Morgan Grant, her husband and Heber's father, had died of pneumonia. Heber was only nine days old.

Heber's father was a well-known pioneer. Jedediah served as Brigham Young's counselor in the First Presidency of the Church; he was the first mayor of Salt Lake City; and he was a general in the territory's Nauvoo Legion. When he died, the members of the Church were sad to lose such a great man. Brigham Young told the mourners at the funeral to have hope. Some other young man would soon come along and ''roar even louder'' than Jedediah—whom Brigham called ''a great lion.'' Could it be that Jedediah's own son, Heber, was that young man?

Heber's road to greatness would not be an easy one. He lived the first seven years of his life on Main Street in Salt Lake City. Luckily, his house was right across the street from the Globe Bakery. The family home, which was shared with several other relatives, was one of the finest in town, with a walk-out balcony, an orchard, a large garden, and plenty of room to romp.

Eventually, however, money troubles forced him and his mother to move out of this lovely home into a small adobe cottage on Second East Street. Here their lives were very different. For furniture they had only a bed and a few chairs. They had six plates (two were cracked) and a few cups and saucers. There were many cold and windy winter nights when Heber and his mother had no fire—and certainly not a furnace—to keep them warm. It was hard to be poor after having lived in such a nice house on Main Street.

Since he was an only child, Heber tried especially hard to help his mother. Rachel earned money by sewing for other people. She also made costumes for the nearby Salt Lake Theatre. At first Rachel sewed clothing by hand. Later she bought a "Wheeler and Wilcox" treadle sewing machine. "I sat on the floor at night until midnight many times," Heber remembered, "and pumped the sewing machine to relieve her tired legs."

Rachel seemed to know Heavenly Father would have a special calling for her son when he grew up. She once told him, "Behave yourself, and you will someday be one of the apostles in the Church." She did everything she could to make sure that he learned the gospel of Jesus Christ and got a good education. Heber, on the other hand, adored his mother and wanted to make her proud of him. They made a great team.

With his mother's help and encouragement, Heber became an excellent student. He was especially good at math and memorization, but he had to work extra hard to get good grades in spelling and foreign languages. President Young took a special interest in Heber and invited him to attend the Young family's private school and join with them in their evening prayers.

Heber's desire to be honest at all times sometimes got him into trouble. One time a teacher asked him about another boy's conduct. Heber told the truth and later received a backyard beating from the misbehaving boy.

Sometimes Heber and his school chums were found doing things they shouldn't. A teacher warned the boys "to stop stealing peaches from the neighborhood gardens." Another time they were told to "quit throwing mud from the end of a stick which disfigured buildings that had cost a great deal."

If one word could describe the future prophet, that word

Rachel Ivins Grant and her son, Heber J., about age ten. Photographer unknown.

would be *persistence*. When Heber made up his mind that there was something he wanted to learn or some way he wanted to improve himself, nothing could stop him from achieving it. His mother seems to have convinced him that the word *can't* just didn't exist.

For instance, Heber loved baseball, but he wasn't very strong and couldn't hit or throw the ball far. He was often called "sissy" or "ramrod" on the playground at school. Heber's long arms and legs caused one boy to refer to him as "that grasshopper dude." Determined to improve, Heber told his mother, "I'm going to play on the ball team that will win the state championship!"

Heber shined forty pairs of shoes to earn money to buy his own baseball. Then, every evening for months he practiced throwing the ball at the side of a barn. To improve his catching, he hired the hardest thrower in school to pitch "bullets" at him. After hours of practice, his arm ached, but Heber was now strong enough and good enough for the best team. To the surprise of many, but not his mother, Heber achieved his goal. He played on the Red Stockings team that won the territorial championship at the end of the season. He became a local hero.

There was another time when Heber showed great determination. Schoolmates teased him for having poor handwriting. "Hentracks!" one boy said. "Lightning has struck the ink bottle," jeered another. Heber vowed to improve. After many hours of practice, he had such beautiful penmanship that people paid him to write holiday and business cards for them. He won a prize for his handwriting and became a professor of penmanship!

Heber and his mother were members of Salt Lake City's Thirteenth Ward, and it was here that his testimony of the gospel was born. Some of the most prominent Church leaders were members of this ward, and Heber loved to hear them speak. He sometimes found himself with tears in his eyes after hearing a humble brother or sister bear testimony of the Prophet

Joseph Smith or tell a miraculous missionary experience. However, if a speaker began to go on too long in sacrament meeting, Heber chuckled to see Bishop Edwin D. Wooley reach out and tug the long-winded preacher on the coattails. That was the signal to sit down.

In Sunday School, Heber and the other children were often divided into teams and asked questions taken from the Bible, Book of Mormon, or Church history. Prizes were given for correct answers.

In one such contest, his uncle Anthony C. Ivins set up a competition between fourteen-year-old Heber and Brother Ivins' own son. A pair of beautiful buckskin gloves was promised to the first one to read the entire Book of Mormon. After the first day, Heber's hopes of winning the gloves were dashed. The Ivins boy had stayed up most of the night and read 150 pages. Heber, who wanted to understand and ponder each verse, had read more slowly and completed only twenty-five pages. But Heber later remembered: "When I finished the book, I not only got a testimony of it . . . but the gloves as well!" After a fast start, his cousin never read another page.

Heber's service to the Church began early. When he was only nineteen years old, he served in the presidency of the first Young Men's program in the Church (Young Men's Improvement Association).

Soon after this, Heber was called to be the president of the Tooele Stake. He was only twenty-three years old—the youngest stake president in the Church at that time. He truly wanted to be a good example for the members of his stake. In his first talk to the stake, he promised:

> I will ask no man in Tooele to be a more honest tithe payer than I will be; I will ask no man to give more of his

Heber J. Grant as a young man, possibly during the years he served in the presidency of the Young Men's program. Photographer unknown.

means in proportion to what he has than I will give; I will ask no man to live the Word of Wisdom better than I live it; and I will give the best that is in me for the benefit of the people in this stake of Zion.

In October 1882, Heber J. Grant was called to be a member of the Council of the Twelve Apostles. He was twenty-five years old. Heber wondered why he had been chosen for such an important calling.

To some it was not a surprise, however. Heber remembered meeting Eliza R. Snow, a prominent leader of the women of the Church, when he was a child. She saw Heber playing on the floor with several other children. She prophesied to those present that "when this child grows to manhood he will become an apostle of the Lord."

And yet, when that prophecy came true, Heber spent several months worrying that he was not worthy to accept the call. He even considered asking the prophet to release him.

Then Heber had an experience that told him his calling was no mistake. He was visiting the Navajo and Hopi Indians in Arizona and decided to leave the main group and ride his mule down a trail alone to pray. As he pleaded for help, Heber "seemed to see and seemed to hear" a special council in heaven:

> The Savior was there, and the Prophet Joseph Smith and my father, Jedediah Grant. It was given to me that the Prophet Joseph Smith and my father requested that I be called. I sat there and wept for joy. And from that day I have never been bothered with the idea that I was not worthy to stand as an apostle.

Fifteen years after becoming an apostle, Heber was called to serve a full-time mission to Japan. While there, he went to a small hill overlooking Yokohama and dedicated the Japanese islands for missionary work. Heber later said that the dedicatory prayer he offered was "the greatest prayer of my life." His companion recalled that "every word penetrated into my very bones and I could have wept with joy." Another companion thought that the ground shook as Elder Grant spoke.

Heber also presided over the British and European Missions and taught the Yaqui Indians in Mexico. In England, his co-workers found him to be "a dynamo of enthusiasm." Heber loved to preach the gospel. "I must do my best to see that everyone in the entire world hears and has a chance to accept the gospel, for it is the key to eternal happiness."

The missionaries loved him. Heber often joined the elders in a game of tennis behind the mission home. One missionary remembered how President Grant used to "whack them over the netting with the speed of a Colt .45!"

Heber was also a family man. He married three wives — Lucy Stringham, Augusta Winters, and Emily Harris Wells — and was the father of twelve children. He had an especially close relationship with his children and grandchildren. "Whenever he was traveling for pleasure or to preach somewhere," his daughter Lucy wrote, "he took some of us along. We loved to go because in our confidential 'travel' chats we got better acquainted and learned to appreciate more fully his great qualities."

When Heber had to leave his family behind, his children remembered how wonderful it was when he returned. "What a jubilant time we had when he came home!" Lucy wrote. "We would all gather around and listen to his experiences. I can see him now walking around the house with a child on each foot, or tossing the children up on his knee!"

When family members had to be away from home, Heber faithfully wrote them letters. When one of Heber's wives was away in a hospital in California, he showered her with letters.

Heber J. Grant in Great Britain in 1914, with his wife Emily Wells and daughters. Photographer unknown.

Lucy remembered, "Almost every day a letter reached mother, and if for some reason it was delayed even the nurses would notice it. I remember the head nurse saying to mother that in all her years of nursing she had never had any man treat his wife as considerately as mother was treated."

In November 1918, President Joseph F. Smith was very ill, and he asked to see Heber, who was next in line to become president of the Church. President Smith reached out, took Heber's hand, and said, "The Lord bless you. You have a great responsibility. Always remember that this is the Lord's work, and not man's. He knows whom He wants to lead His Church, and He will bless you." Less than a week later, President Smith died, and Heber Jeddy Grant became the Church's seventh prophet, seer, and revelator.

Early in his presidency, Heber J. Grant dedicated the first temples built in the twentieth century. He dedicated the Hawaiian Temple in 1919, the Alberta Temple in 1923, and the Arizona Temple in 1927.

In the early 1930s, America was stricken with a terrible financial depression. Money was scarce. Many people lost their jobs and property. Some people were nearly starving. Many came to "soup kitchens" to receive a bowl of soup or piece of bread. Even skilled workers could find no one to hire them. Those who could work were paid much less than they had earned before the Great Depression.

President Grant was a wise businessman and saw the need to organize a plan to help the Saints. In 1936, he started a security plan that later became the Church Welfare Program. To help the plan succeed, he donated his large dry farm in western Utah, which was worth more than eighty thousand dollars. President Grant worked with national political leaders and banks to keep important Utah- and Church-owned businesses open. He led both the Church and community through this very difficult time.

After becoming a very successful banker and insurance salesman, President Grant kept a promise he had made to himself years earlier to share with the poor. Remembering his own moth-

The First Presidency, 1934–1945. Heber J. Grant is standing center. J. Reuben Clark, Jr., first counselor, is to the left; David O. McKay, second counselor, is to the right. Photographer unknown.

er's struggles, he took special delight in helping widows. He came to the aid of many who were behind in their house payments. He helped pay their bills and often enclosed enough additional money for a small personal gift. He gave many young couples money to help pay medical expenses for the birth of a new baby.

President Grant fed the hungry, as the Savior taught; he traveled many miles to help someone in need and gave away thousands of books and pamphlets to friends and business partners. This man, who as a youth was a baseball hero, thus became a hero of an even greater kind.

When asked once if he had any advice to give to young boys and girls, he replied, "Yes, tell them to make others happy and to aid them in carrying their burdens in life. Then they will be sure of happiness, not only in their lives here, but in the life to come."

President Heber J. Grant died on May 15, 1945, at age eighty-eight. He was buried in the Salt Lake Cemetery across the road from his father, whom he had never known—but who surely was very proud of his son who had become a prophet of the Lord.

George Albert Smith

A Solemn Promise Not to Be
an Enemy to Anyone

Young George Albert Smith was a daredevil. After a snow-storm left a heavy blanket of snow on his hometown, Salt Lake City, George could hardly wait to grab his wooden sled and go "coasting." As far as he was concerned, the *steeper* the hill and the *slicker* the ice the better. Once, he coasted down a city street at such breakneck speed (he loved to go fast!) that he lost control of his sled, ran into a tall gas street lamp, and got a gash that scarred his forehead the rest of his life. There were no cars in those days for coasters to worry about, but obviously one had to watch out for gas lamps!

George Albert was a happy boy who loved to make people laugh. He and his buddies Wilby Dougall and Tom Peck staged musical variety shows in back of the Smith barn. For an ad-mission price of a few pennies, neighborhood children and their parents could watch George Albert stroll out in his homemade suit and big cowboy hat. With funny songs and jokes, he sent his audience into fits of laughter. One favorite song was this:

> I'm not very handsome, I know that I'm not.
> I'm as ugly as sin, and ought to be shot.

119

My mouth is a feature that can't be forgot—
If you travel east, west, north or south.

Chorus: Shut it! Shut it! Don't open it quite so wide.
Shut it! Shut it! I don't want to get inside.

Once a lady in his audience laughed so hard after hearing this song she nearly fainted.

The future prophet was also adventurous. While still a small boy, George Albert decided he wanted to see his grandpa and grandma Farr who lived north of Salt Lake City in Ogden. He grabbed a playmate, and together they walked a half mile to the railroad station and climbed aboard a train that was headed north. The problem was . . . they hadn't asked their mothers. Luckily, the train conductor spied them, stopped the train before it left the station, and sent the boys home. Their mothers were not pleased.

George Albert Smith was born April 4, 1870, the second of the eleven children born to John Henry Smith and Sarah Farr. When he wasn't putting on neighborhood variety shows or hopping on trains bound for Ogden, George Albert had work to do. He had horses and cows to feed, wood to haul and chop, crops to plant and harvest, and buggies to wash and grease.

In addition to his chores at home, George Albert began working for ZCMI (a Church-owned department store) when he was thirteen years old. He earned $2.50 a week putting buttons on overalls. He later made packing boxes. George was a hard worker and often raced to see if he could get more work done than his coworkers. He once made one hundred boxes in one day. The most any of the other workers could put together was sixty.

George Albert also went the extra mile to get the attention of the girls in his neighborhood. Actually, he was interested in one girl and one girl only—Lucy Woodruff. She was the grand-

George Albert Smith, about age three. Photograph by C. R. Savage, ca. 1873

daughter of Wilford Woodruff, who would become president of the Church when George Albert was nineteen. Because of the death of her mother, Lucy lived with her grandparents just down the street from the Smith family.

George Albert's first attempts to impress Lucy didn't go so smoothly. He decided that the only way to get her attention was to tease her, which he did mercilessly. Once, when Lucy was walking past the Smith home with a pail full of yeast, George dashed out and teased her until she spilled the yeast on the ground. Another time he tied her to a tree with her long brown braids. At school he dipped her braids in an ink well! If George Albert was trying to make friends with Lucy Woodruff, it just wasn't working. It was time for a different approach—and George had an idea.

Most of the other families in the neighborhood were far wealthier than the Smith's and had lush green lawns on which to hold summer dances and parties. With the help of his brothers and sisters, George Albert worked for months putting in a front lawn to make their yard more appealing to the other youngsters in the area—especially to Lucy Woodruff. Besides, since his father was in Europe on a mission, the lawn would be a delightful surprise upon his return.

After more than a year of back-breaking work (raking, earning money for top-quality seed, planting, watering, and tending the first tiny green shoots) a beautiful lawn soon covered the Smith yard. Upon his return, George's father was thrilled. And, more importantly, Lucy Woodruff and her grandparents took notice. They stopped by the Smith home after Sunday School one day, and Lucy was overheard to say, "George, your family has the most beautiful front yard in the entire ward. I should like to sit under your apple tree whenever you will let me." The Woodruffs were invited to stay that afternoon. The adults sat on lawn chairs while the young folks sat on a quilt. George's mother served them all lemon ice cream and sponge cake. George was bursting with pride. The plan had worked!

A few years later, George Albert impressed Lucy in another way. The two of them were sitting on her grandmother's porch in a swing facing Temple Square when a hot air balloon came floating by, dangerously low. George Albert suddenly jumped up and shouted, "I think that balloon is going to hit the Tabernacle!" And indeed it did! The balloon instantly burst into flames, starting a small fire on the roof of the Tabernacle.

George didn't stand around trying to decide what to do. He raced to the nearest telephone and called the fire department. The engines soon arrived, but they couldn't get inside Temple Square. The gate was locked, and the night watchman didn't have a key. George Albert and several other men formed a straight line and charged the gate. It finally burst open when they hit it with all their might. Everyone worked together to put the fire out before the building was seriously damaged. George had acted quickly to help save the Tabernacle from being destroyed by fire. How proud Lucy was of him!

Where did George Albert get all his courage? Where did he learn to work so hard, think so quickly, and get things done?

For one thing, George Albert grew up in a neighborhood full of courageous people—some of them relatives. When George Albert was born, President Brigham Young lived just two blocks away in the Lion House. The streets near the Smith home (at 23 North West Temple) were lined with the homes of apostles of the Church, Relief Society and Primary presidents, great missionaries, and other hearty pioneers.

For example, George's grandfather George A. Smith (whose name he proudly shared) lived next door and was a member of the First Presidency of the Church. This kindly man was a cousin to the Prophet Joseph Smith and one of his closest friends. George A. was a "big grandpa" (weighing over three hundred pounds), and he wore a wig that once blew away during a stiff wind storm. When he removed his wig and false teeth one time in front of a group of Indians, they ran away in terror, thinking he had some sort of magical powers. George's other grandfather

Construction of the Salt Lake Temple in 1875, with Tabernacle to the right. George Albert Smith lived on West Temple Street, to the right of the Tabernacle. Photographer unknown.

Lorin Farr was the first mayor of Ogden and the first stake president in Weber County.

But the two people George Albert admired most were his parents, Sarah Farr and John Henry Smith. His mother was a gentle and deeply spiritual woman who ran a loving, tidy household. John Henry Smith was an apostle and a member of the First Presidency of the Church. George often said he had never known a better or greater man than his father.

George Albert was born and reared right across the street from Temple Square, and he grew up hearing the sounds of the magnificent temple being built. Work on the Salt Lake Temple was begun long before George was born, and it was not dedicated until he was twenty-three years old. So throughout his youth, he could hear constant hammering, sawing, and stonecutting from across the street. Ox carts—sometimes fifty at a time—were continually arriving at Temple Square, bringing stone from the rock quarry in Little Cottonwood Canyon.

When George Albert was a toddler, the temple walls were just above the ground level. And as the walls grew in height and strength, so did the future prophet's testimony of the gospel. The strength of that testimony blessed his life on many occasions. While still a small child, for example, he came down with typhoid fever. The doctor recommended he be kept in bed and given only coffee to drink. But George Albert had been taught the importance of the Word of Wisdom and refused the doctor's advice. Instead, he asked to be administered to by one of their home teachers. He received a beautiful blessing from this poor but faithful man, and George Albert recovered almost immediately. The doctor was amazed to see him playing outside with his friends the next day.

As the temple walls continued to rise even higher, George Albert's family helped bring him close to his Heavenly Father. He was still a small child when his mother first taught him to pray:

> I remember mother took me by the hand, led me up the stairs into the bedroom where my crib was, and sitting by my crib, she had me kneel. She took both my little hands in hers and taught me how to pray. Young as I was, that prayer went through me, and I felt confidence in it. I felt secure.

Having been taught the importance of prayer, George Albert

knew just what to do when one day a heavy kitchen cupboard toppled over, knocking his mother to the floor. He couldn't revive her and feared she had been killed. He knelt down and begged his Father in Heaven to save her life. With tears in his eyes, he promised the Lord he would devote his life to preaching the gospel and doing the Lord's will if only his mother would be saved. Sarah Smith was healed, and George kept his promise.

When George Albert was fourteen years old, and the Salt Lake Temple had risen to a magnificent eighty feet, he was given his patriarchal blessing. It included the following promises:

> Thy voice shall be as the voice of a trumpet in declaring the words of the Lord to the nobles of the earth, and many shall believe in thy words and embrace the gospel of the Son of God. . . . Thou art called to do a great and mighty work in the great kingdoms of God . . . and *thou shalt become a mighty prophet* in the midst of the sons of Zion. Thou art destined to become a mighty man before the Lord, for thou shalt become *a mighty apostle* in the Church and kingdom of God upon the earth, for none of thy father's family shall have more power with God than thou shalt have, for none shall excel thee.

While George Albert's spiritual knowledge was growing, he was also learning his ABCs at school. He first attended the old Brigham Young School on South Temple Street and then the Seventeenth Ward School. In those days most wards had their own school.

But all was not long-faced and serious. George Albert still loved to make people laugh. One day as the teacher was about to leave the classroom, she said to the class, "Don't any of you leave your seats!" As soon as she left, George Albert picked up his chair and paraded around the room. Upon the teacher's

George Albert Smith (right), about sixteen, when he was attending Brigham Young Academy, with friend John Howard. Photograph attributed to George E. Anderson, ca. 1886.

return, some of the students complained that George Albert had left his seat. When the teacher asked him if this were true, he replied, "No, indeed, I didn't. I took it with me!"

During his teenage years, George Albert lived with relatives in Provo while he attended the Brigham Young Academy. George did especially well in spelling and grammar, but one teacher said his penmanship "could be improved."

George Albert worked for three years as a traveling salesman for ZCMI. Together with a companion named Jim, he would travel throughout Utah visiting stores in smaller towns, taking orders for merchandise from Salt Lake City. George wanted to be a good salesman and get as many orders as he could.

One day, while in Heber City, George Albert was told by a friend that one of the other salesmen had gotten ahead of him and was already across the mountain in Park City. Those were George's customers! Rather than get in his horse-drawn buggy and go around the mountain the long way, he decided to take a shortcut.

George Albert checked his horse in at a livery stable and rented a bicycle. He pushed his bicycle to the top of the hill that separated the two communities, went over the top, climbed aboard the bicycle, and raced down the other side of the hill as fast as the bicycle would go. Unfortunately, he discovered partway down the hill that the bicycle had no brakes! Looking for a way to stop, he spied a huge clump of thick bushes and decided to steer the bicycle into them. The bushes did, indeed, stop the bicycle. They also tore George Albert's clothing to pieces. He later told a relative: "I was willing to do almost anything to stay ahead of the competition."

George Albert was aspiring to become an officer in the Utah State Guard when an incident of great importance took place. He lost his bid to become an officer, he believed, because a rival spread ugly rumors about him. George felt such anger toward the man that he felt like physically attacking him. He couldn't even bring himself to take the sacrament at church because his heart was filled with so much anger. But George Albert prayed to his Father in Heaven for help. He finally decided to go directly to the man and ask for forgiveness because of the ill feelings he had felt towards him. The rumormonger felt deep regret for his actions, also begged for forgiveness, and the two men shook hands and became lifelong friends.

His desire to love all people became a theme in George Albert's life. He made a solemn promise "not to be an enemy to any living soul." Everyone who knew George Albert agreed that he kept that promise throughout his life.

Eighteen ninety-two, when George Albert was twenty-two years old, proved to be a very important year. In April, the capstone of the Salt Lake Temple was put in place during a special ceremony. The temple was now as tall as it was going to be, and the time had come to finish the interior so the Temple could be dedicated.

By now George Albert had grown to young manhood, and he, too, was as tall as he was going to be. It was time to form his own family. On May 25, George Albert married his childhood sweetheart, Lucy Woodruff, in the Manti Temple. As a wedding gift, Lucy gave her husband a beautiful gold locket set with diamonds. Inside the locket were two pictures of Lucy: one of her as a young girl, and the other as his new bride. George Albert treasured this locket and wore it nearly every day of his life.

Soon after the wedding, George was called to serve a mission to Chattanooga, Tennessee. At first, he served alone, without his new bride. But Lucy missed him terribly and received permission to join him in the mission field a few months later.

On one occasion before Lucy joined him, George Albert and

his mission president were sleeping in a house in Alabama when an angry mob surrounded the house. They fired shots through the windows several times, but they aimed too high, and the bullets flew by just above the missionaries' heads! George Albert later told Lucy:

> Splinters were flying over our heads in every direction. But I felt absolutely no terror. I was very calm as I lay there, experiencing one of the most horrible events of my life, but I was sure that as long as I was preaching the word of God and following his teachings that the Lord would protect me. And he did.

After the mission, George Albert and Lucy returned to Salt Lake City where he worked for the government and served in many Church callings. He especially loved the scouting program and was awarded scouting's highest honor—the Silver Buffalo Award. Throughout his life George Albert was proud to wear his well-pressed Boy Scout uniform on special occasions.

As a loyal Scout, George Albert believed in treating others with kindness, whether or not he was wearing the Scout uniform. His granddaughter Martha Stewart Hatch tells of how he handled one difficult situation in his neighborhood with great wisdom:

> Once on a hot summer day there was some problem happening under the street near Grandfather's home in Salt Lake City, and some workers from the city had come to fix it. It was hot outdoors, the sun shone fiercely, and the job at hand was a pick-and-shovel kind that made the sweat pour off the men's faces and backs as they dug into the roadway. The workers were not careful with their language, or maybe their mothers hadn't taught them any better, but they were swearing and using terrible language. Their words soon became offensive to many of the neighbors whose

windows were open to catch any breeze that might help to cool them.

Someone went out and asked the men to stop their foul talk, and in the process pointed out that Brother Smith lived right there—couldn't they show some respect and keep quiet, please? With that the men let loose a new string of bad words. Quietly, Grandfather prepared some lemonade and placing some glasses and the pitcher on a tray he carried it out to the struggling men with, "My friends, you look so hot and tired. Why don't you come and sit under my trees here and have a cool drink?" Their anger gone, the men responded to the kindness with meekness and appreciation. After their pleasant little break they went back to their labor and finished their work carefully and quietly.

When George Albert was thirty-three years old, he got the biggest surprise of his life. On Saturday, October 6, 1903, he couldn't get a seat in the Tabernacle to attend general conference, so he took his two daughters, Edith and Emily, to the state fair—something he had been promising to do for several days. The girls especially wanted to see "the little pink pigs." When they returned home, they found a whole crowd of people standing on their front lawn, hugging and kissing Lucy and congratulating her. George Albert wondered what on earth had happened. "What is this all about?" he asked.

"Don't you know?" a neighbor lady asked, surprised that he hadn't heard. "You were just sustained in conference as a member of the Quorum of the Twelve Apostles."

George Albert couldn't believe it! At first he felt unworthy to be an apostle. He wondered if he was ready for such an important calling. He also did not have good health. He often had to stay at home or rest in bed because he was so tired and weak. Many times he wished his body were stronger so he could

George Albert Smith's wife, Lucy Woodruff, and their daughters Edith (left) and Emily (right). Photograph by Johnson Company of Salt Lake City, 1909.

George Albert Smith with son, George Albert, Jr. Photographer unknown, 1909.

accomplish even more. But he loved his Heavenly Father and would gladly do his best to serve him.

The Lord knew George Albert loved all people. He continued to live faithfully by his promise "not to be an enemy to any living soul." As an apostle, George Albert showed special concern for those who were lonely and poor. He often spent Christmas day in the poorest part of town, visiting those everyone else had forgotten. One of his daughters, Emily Smith Stewart, wrote of how they spent Christmas day:

> Father always took us with him to make the rounds of the forgotten friends that he habitually visited on Christmas. I was a very little girl and I remember going down a long

alley in the middle of a city block where there were some very poor houses. We opened the door of one tiny home and there on the bed lay an old woman, very sad and alone. As we came in, tears ran down her cheeks, and she reached over to take hold of Father's hand as we gave her our little remembrances. "I am grateful to you for coming," she said, "because if you hadn't come I would have no Christmas at all. No one else has remembered me."

Another Christmas years later, his now-married children gave him a new winter coat to replace the worn and tattered one he had been wearing to work at the Church Office Building. A couple of weeks later, on a bitterly cold day, one of his daughters picked him up at his office to bring him home. She noticed he was wearing his old coat again.

"Where's that beautiful new winter coat we gave you for Christmas, Papa?" she asked. At first President Smith refused to answer. Finally he said, "An elderly gentleman visited me in my office today. He had no coat and was so cold he was almost blue. He needed a coat so badly, so I gave him mine."

"But why didn't you give him your old coat?" his daughter asked. President Smith replied, "Oh, he needed that new coat much more than I did."

A great sorrow came to George Albert in 1937 when his loving wife, Lucy, died. He lived fourteen more years after her death but he never remarried, even as he rose to the very helm of the Church.

After serving as an apostle for forty-two years, George Albert Smith became the eighth president of the Church in 1945. He was president only six years, and he still suffered from poor health, but he accomplished very important things in that short time.

World War II ended just six days before George Albert became prophet of the Church. That terrible war left millions of people in Europe without homes, food, or clothing. George Albert wanted to help. He met with the president of the United States, Harry Truman, to ask for the government's help in shipping donated supplies to the people of Europe. President Truman agreed to help but asked, "You mean you're just going to give them the food and clothing for free?" President Smith replied, "Of course we would give it to them! They are our brothers and sisters and are in distress! God has blessed us with a surplus and we will be glad to send it."

As president of the Church, George Albert Smith dedicated the Idaho Falls Temple and in 1947 presided over the celebration of the one hundredth anniversary of the arrival of the pioneers in the Salt Lake Valley. He pulled the rope that unveiled the "This Is the Place Monument." At April Conference in 1950, President Smith rejoiced in announcing that the total Church membership had reached the one million mark.

But most important of all, President Smith pleaded with members of the Church to understand how important the gospel is and encouraged them to love each other and live good lives. Near the end of his life he said:

> I can think of nobody who has had a fuller life than I have had, and I don't say that boastfully, but gratefully; and I want to say to you that every happiness and every joy has been the result of keeping the commandments of God and observing his advice and counsel.

President Smith never lost the wonderful sense of humor he had as a boy. Whenever he was having dinner with his grandchildren, for instance, he loved to hide their dessert under the table or on a nearby shelf while they were busy carrying dishes into the kitchen. His impish grin and charming blue eyes would

George Albert Smith, about age forty-three. Photographer unknown, ca. 1913.

tell them their grandfather had been up to some mischief with their food again.

President Smith loved children and had small chairs and toys in his office in the Church Office Building. This gave his small visitors something to do while he talked with their parents. This dignified, neatly groomed man often held a jump rope for the neighborhood children while they played on the sidewalk in front of his home.

In the end it could truly be said that President Smith remained faithful to his creed. He was loved by young and old and had not an enemy in the world.

President Smith died on his eighty-first birthday in 1951. As he died he held in his hand the gold locket Lucy had given him on their wedding day, fifty-nine years earlier.

George Albert Smith with Boy Scout Jimmy McFarland by This Is the Place Monument. Photograph attributed to Clarence Williams.

David O. McKay

A Boy Who Had Something to Do Besides Play Marbles

Emma Ray Riggs was attending a family reunion when she heard that a friend of hers, whom she hadn't seen for two years, would soon be arriving in Salt Lake City. Emma Ray, or "Ray" as everyone called her, wanted to be at the train station to meet him, but the reunion was being held on a cattle ranch on Antelope Island in the middle of the Great Salt Lake. No bridge connected the island with the shore.

The passenger boat that had brought Ray and her cousin Belle to the island would not be returning in time. So the two of them rigged a sail on an old rowboat and took turns pulling on the oars to get to shore and into town to meet this special person.

Ray's friend was a twenty-six-year-old returning missionary, David Oman McKay, who had been in Great Britain preaching the gospel. The handsome, six-foot one-inch Elder was anxious see his family . . . and Ray.

David O. and Ray not only had a happy reunion that August day in 1899, but their friendship soon blossomed into romance. They were married January 2, 1901, and had the honor of being the first couple married in the Salt Lake Temple in the twentieth century.

When they first met, Ray was smitten by David O.'s tall athletic build, his handsome features, and piercing hazel-brown eyes. She would soon discover that he had inner qualities that were even more important. He was courteous, for instance. He insisted on opening all doors for her, he helped her with her coat, and always stood up when she entered the room. He also had a wonderful sense of humor and loved good books.

But there was a lot more to David O. McKay than just a handsome face and a pleasing personality. The eye of the Lord was on David O., and he would have an important work to do. From their wedding day on, and for the next sixty-nine years, Emma Ray Riggs McKay would be at her husband's side helping him accomplish that work.

David Oman McKay was born September 8, 1873, on his family's farm in Huntsville, Utah. He was the third of ten children born to David and Jennette Evans McKay, Latter-day Saint emigrants from Scotland and Wales.

The McKay home was filled with love, but the family suffered their share of sadness and disappointment. Tragedy struck in 1880, when David O.'s two older sisters died the same week and were buried in a common grave. David O. was now the oldest child in the family and his parents would depend on him to help even more at home and with the farm work.

This became especially true a year later when David O.'s father was unexpectedly called on a mission to Scotland. While his father was away, seven-year-old David O. became "the man of the house," milking cows, feeding the livestock, and doing household chores for his mother.

Before he went to college, David O. took on a summer job to bring extra income to the family. He became a newspaper

David and Jennette McKay Family, ca. 1877. The children from left to right are Ellen, David O., Thomas, and Margaret. Photographer unknown.

boy and carried the *Ogden Standard* to La Plata, a nearby mining town. He rode his horse all the way, and the round trip took him from seven in the morning to five o'clock in the evening.

During this time David O. read books, memorized poems and quotes from great literature, and became more familiar with the scriptures. Some of the passages he memorized while riding his horse would be heard years later in sermons he would give in general conference and other Church meetings.

David O. learned early, by experience, to trust in his Heavenly Father. It brought him comfort when he was afraid:

When [I was] a very young child in the home of my youth, I was fearful at night. . . .

One night I could not sleep, and I fancied I heard noises around the house. Mother was away in another room. Thomas E. [my younger brother] by my side was sleeping soundly. I became terribly [fearful], and I decided to pray as my parents had taught me. I thought I could only pray by getting out of bed and kneeling, and that was a terrible test.

But I did finally bring myself to get out of bed and kneel and pray to God to protect Mother and the family. And a voice as [clear] to me as mine is to you said, "Don't be afraid. Nothing will hurt you." Where it came from, what it was, I am not saying. You may judge. To me it was a direct answer, and there came an assurance that I should never be hurt in bed at night.

In 1885, David O. became known as "the bishop's oldest son" when his father was made bishop of their Huntsville ward. That same year, David O. was ordained a deacon in the Aaronic Priesthood. He helped his quorum with many projects like cleaning the chapel for Church meetings and chopping wood for the widows in their ward.

When he was thirteen, David O. received his patriarchal blessing from John Smith, patriarch to the Church. The blessing contained important clues to the young man's future life. Among other things, the patriarch said:

Thou art in thy youth and need instruction, therefore I say unto thee, be taught of thy parents the way of life and salvation, that at an early day you may be prepared for a responsible position. *The Lord has a work for thee to do, in which thou shalt see much of the world,* assist in gathering scattered Israel and also labor in the ministry. It shall be thy lot to sit in council with thy brethren and preside among the people and exhort the Saints to faithfulness.

When the blessing was finished, the kindly patriarch put his hands on David O.'s already muscular shoulders and said, "My boy, you have something to do in this life besides playing marbles." At first, David O. didn't understand what the patriarch meant by that comment. David O. went into the kitchen where his mother was preparing dinner and said, "If he thinks I'm going to stop playing marbles, he is mistaken!" But his wise mother explained that what he meant was that the things David O. was interested in now—like marbles and other boyhood games—would someday be put aside as he grew to manhood and became involved in much more important tasks.

David O. absolutely loved school. He enjoyed being in the classroom so much, in fact, that he decided he wanted to become a teacher. After completing the eighth grade in Huntsville, he attended the Church-owned Weber Stake Academy in Ogden. He was only twenty years old when he was asked to serve as principal of the school in Huntsville. However, he declined.

David O. needed more education. He attended the University of Utah, where he graduated as valedictorian—an honor given to the best student. David O. was well-liked, and he was voted president of his class. When he wasn't studying, he played left guard on that school's first-ever football team.

Like his father, David O. received a surprise mission call from the Church to the British Isles. It was time to move on to one of those "more important tasks" his mother said would be in his future. David O. walked some of the same paths his father had walked as a missionary in the British Isles some sixteen years earlier.

The first University of Utah football team, 1894. David O. McKay is standing second from the left. Photographer unknown.

As a boy, long before he became a missionary, David O. had prayed often for some kind of special manifestation or experience that would tell him the Church was true. For years, he had received no answer to those prayers. He became discouraged and wondered if Heavenly Father was really listening. But he was patient, and his answer finally did come while he was on his mission.

During a special priesthood meeting in Scotland, David O. felt the Holy Ghost so strongly he had tears in his eyes. One missionary stood up and said he felt the presence of angels in the room. The mission president, James L. McMurrin, turned to David O. in the meeting and said, "Let me tell you, Brother David, Satan hath desired you that he may sift you as wheat, but God is mindful of you. If you will keep the faith, you will yet sit in the leading councils of the Church."

For David O. the strong spirit present in the room that day was a sign of God's love and concern for him. He felt special gratitude for the missionaries who years earlier had converted his grandparents in Scotland and Wales to the gospel. From that day forward, he fully committed himself to serving his Heavenly Father and his fellow men—no matter how great the sacrifice.

But there was a career to begin and a family to raise before his mission president's prophecy would be fulfilled. After David O. returned home from his mission, he married Ray (whom he had met at the University of Utah), and they made their home in Ogden. There he became a popular school teacher and administrator, serving later as principal of the Weber Stake Academy. He was the sort of principal who made sure things got done. He raised money to pay for a new addition on to the school building, started a student newspaper, began a popular lecture series, and organized and directed a school band. The students and townspeople liked him very much.

David O.'s talent as a teacher was valuable to the Church. He wrote lesson material for his ward and stake Sunday School classes. He helped others become better teachers. Many of his suggestions for Sunday Schools in Ogden were later adopted by the whole Church.

David O. and Ray became the parents of seven children. During family times they enjoyed playing games like Rook, Pit, and backgammon, riding in their horse-drawn sleigh with the sound of jingling bells filling the air, and playing musical instruments.

David O. and Emma Ray McKay enjoying music.

David O. and Ray never spanked their children but certainly expected to be obeyed. Their son David Lawrence remembers how one incident was handled:

> We were riding to Huntsville one time in the surrey (a horse-drawn carriage). Llewelyn and I were scuffling in the back seat. This was dangerous because it would have been easy for a youngster to fall out in front of the rear wheel. Father asked us to stop playing. We kept on. The next thing I knew (Father arranged it so that suddenly) I was walking, watching the surrey getting farther and farther away up the hill as I trudged along behind. I started running for Huntsville. Fortunately, Father and the surrey were waiting for me at the top of the hill. Llewelyn and I were quiet the rest of the way.

David O. loved animals—especially horses. Even during these busy years as a principal in Ogden he would find time to get up early in the morning, drive the thirteen miles to the farm in Huntsville to help break in a new colt, and then be back in Ogden by the time school began. In later life, he had a favorite riding horse called Sonny Boy.

David O. wanted his children to love animals too and to take good care of their pets. Once the family had started off for a Fourth of July celebration in Huntsville. A mile or two down the road, David O. asked one of his sons if he had fed his pet rabbits that morning. He said no, he had forgotten. They turned around and went back to the farm so the son could take care of that important chore.

When David O. McKay was thirty-two years old, the words of his patriarchal blessing and those of his mission president were fulfilled. He was called to be a member of the Quorum of the Twelve Apostles.

David O. McKay and his favorite horse, Sonny Boy. Photographer unknown.

For several years, David O. and Ray remained in their home in Ogden, where David O. continued as principal of the Weber Stake Academy. Since his work as an apostle required him to be in Salt Lake City a few days each week, he spent a lot of time riding the "Bamberger," a train that ran between Salt Lake City and Ogden.

During these years David O. was often away from home. One night when he was home for dinner for the first time in several weeks, David O. complimented his wife on the fine meal. After Ray thanked him, their four-year-old daughter Lou Jean piped up with "Come again. Good-bye."

As an apostle, David O. served the Lord in many ways. He was general superintendent of the Sunday School, Church commissioner of education, and president of the European Mission for two years. Later, David O. served as counselor in the First Presidency to two prophets—Heber J. Grant and George Albert Smith. This service helped prepare him for the calling that lay ahead.

On April 9, 1951, David Oman McKay was sustained as the ninth president of the Church. During the nineteen years he served as prophet, the Church grew by leaps and bounds. The number of Latter-day Saints more than doubled to nearly three million members. The number of missionaries grew from two thousand to eighteen thousand. He dedicated temples in Switzerland, London, Los Angeles, Oakland, and New Zealand. Nearly four thousand Church buildings were constructed. The number of stakes grew from 184 to 500.

President McKay traveled over a million miles throughout the world, inspiring the Saints and making friends for the Church among government leaders. This man, who as a boy loved to play with marbles and delivered newspapers on horseback, was now visiting heads of state and royal families. During a visit with the queen of the Netherlands, he showed how he was able to make friends without sacrificing his religious beliefs:

> [The queen] had scheduled a half hour for a visit with President and Sister McKay. He carefully watched the time. When the half hour was up, he politely thanked the queen and began to leave. "Mr. McKay," she said, "sit down! I have enjoyed this thirty minutes more than I have enjoyed any thirty minutes in a long time. I just wish you would extend our visit a little longer." After more persuasion from her, he sat down again. At that point a coffee table was wheeled in, and the queen poured three cups of tea, pushing

one each to President and Mrs. McKay. When neither of
the McKays began to stir their tea, the queen asked,
"Won't you have a little tea with the queen?" No,
President McKay explained, the Latter-day Saints did not
believe in drinking stimulants, and they believed tea to
be a stimulant. "I am the queen of the Netherlands," she
responded. "Do you mean to tell me you won't have a
little drink of tea, even with the queen of the
Netherlands?" "Would the queen of the Netherlands ask
the leader of one million, three hundred thousand people
to do something that he teaches his people not to do?" he
asked in return. "You are a great man, President McKay,"
she replied. "I wouldn't ask you to do that."

President McKay used two phrases during his presidency
that have become mottos for the whole Church: "Every
member a missionary" and "No success can compensate for
failure in the home." He also encouraged the Saints in other
countries to "Stay where you are" and make the Church
strong abroad rather than emigrating to Utah.

President McKay will be remembered for these things, but
his personal qualities were what caused the people he led to
love him dearly. President McKay had a special love for children. One time, at the close of a stake conference in
California, he said, "After the closing prayer, I would like all
the children to meet me back in the cultural hall so I can
shake their hands." True to his promise, the tall, robust,
white-haired prophet spent nearly an hour after the meeting
shaking the hands of the children and chatting with them.

Another quality was President McKay's wonderful sense
of humor. One day while climbing a hill to inspect a site for a
chapel, two local Church officers reached out to help him,
one on either arm. Partway up the hill, President McKay

David O. McKay driving a sleigh near his Huntsville home. Photographer unknown.

stopped and said, "Brethren, I don't mind helping one of you climb this hill, but I can't carry you both."

President McKay died on January 18, 1970, at the age of ninety-six. He had lived longer than any other president of the Church.

The author Robert Louis Stevenson wrote a tribute that very easily could have been written in honor of President David Oman McKay:

> He has achieved success who has lived well, laughed often, and loved much, who has gained the respect of intelligent men and the love of little children, who has filled his niche and accomplished his task, who has left the world better than he found it.

David O. McKay, about age eighty-five. Photographer unknown, ca. 1958.

Joseph Fielding Smith

Historian, Author, Pie-maker

Nobody was allowed to call Joseph Fielding Smith, Jr., "Joe." Not his playmates. Not his brothers and sisters. Not his teachers.

Joseph shared his name with four deeply loved ancestors, including his father (Joseph F., sixth president of the Church) and his granduncle (the Prophet Joseph Smith). The name "Joseph" was almost sacred to his family, and no one was permitted to shorten it. So, Joseph it was, and Joseph it stayed.

Julina Lambson Smith, mother of the future prophet, knew from the whisperings of the Holy Ghost that her son would have a high calling in life. She promised the Lord that if she were blessed with a healthy son, she would raise him to be worthy and prepare him to spend his life in service to members of the Church. Her prayers were answered, and Joseph Fielding was born on July 19, 1876, a hot dry day in Salt Lake City. He was born during the tenth year of his parents' marriage and was often called their "tithing child."

From the time Joseph Fielding was old enough to hold something in his hands, he loved to read. "I used to read the books that were prepared for the Primary children and for Sunday

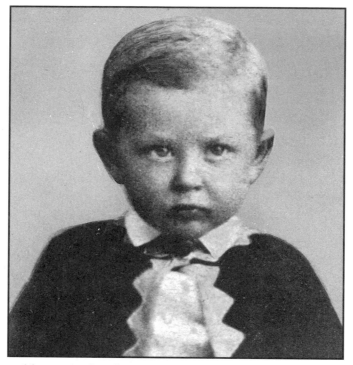

Joseph Fielding Smith, about age three. Photographer unknown, ca. 1879.

School children in those early days," he said. "I usually had a book in my hands when I was home."

If he suddenly disappeared, Joseph Fielding could usually be found in the hayloft or sitting in the shade of the poplar tree in front of the Smith home on Third West. Of course his face was buried in a book. He loved to play baseball with his brothers, but when their games were over, Joseph Fielding soon went back to his books. He read the Book of Mormon twice before he was ordained a deacon.

Perhaps Joseph Fielding would dream under that poplar tree of writing a book himself someday, one that the Saints would love to read. That dream would come true. In fact this bright little bookworm would eventually publish twenty-five books.

But Joseph Fielding could not spend all day dreaming of books. There was work to be done. And considering the size of the Smith family, they had more work to do than most. Joseph Fielding's father had five wives and forty-two children, and everyone needed food, clothing, and shelter . . . and love.

His parents saw to it that Joseph Fielding received plenty of love and attention, but the family had to do without many material things that others would call "necessities of life." When he needed new boots, for instance, his father would take him to the general store and trade his old pair for a new pair. Well, they weren't exactly "new"—they were just larger. No doubt, some other child had worn the boots until they pinched his toes. Then that pair was traded in and left at the store for some other youngster to use. Lucky was the child who had brand-new winter boots.

Joseph Fielding's boyhood years were trying times for the Church. The United States government and most people outside the Church did not share the Latter-day Saints' belief in plural marriage. They threatened to take away Church property and the voting rights of the Saints if the Church continued to teach and practice it.

Day and night, federal marshals searched on horseback for men who had more than one wife. They broke into people's homes without permission, questioning children and wives about where the father of the family was. They searched the house for possible hideouts. If found, the men were arrested and put in jail. Sometimes Joseph Fielding's father had to hide for months at a time to avoid being arrested.

These were often frightening years for young Joseph Fielding. He didn't see his father very much and turned to his mother for comfort and companionship. Julina was a hardworking woman who dressed in simple but attractive clothing and wore her hair pulled back into a bun on the back of her head. She had a friendly, outgoing personality and enjoyed entertaining friends in their home. She is the only woman who was the wife of one president of the Church and the mother of another.

When Joseph Fielding was ten years old, Julina gave him a new responsibility that taught him the importance of serving others. Julina studied medicine and became a midwife—one who delivers babies. As soon as she received word that a baby was on the way, Joseph Fielding became her "right-hand man." He was sent to the stable to get their mare, "Old Meg." He would stand on a box to get the harness on her and the bit in her mouth and then hitch her to the buggy and drive Julina to the home of the expectant mother.

The two of them often traveled on muddy, rutted roads and in rain, sleet, and blowing snow in the open buggy. Julina's brown leather satchel full of medical tools was always tucked safely down by their feet. It seemed to young Joseph Fielding that too many babies decided to come in the middle of the night. Even that inconvenience helped Julina teach Joseph, by example, the importance of service whenever and wherever needed.

Over a period of eighteen years, Julina helped bring nearly a thousand babies safely into the world! Usually she was paid $6.00 for delivering a baby and caring for the mother and child for five or six days. However, many times she served without charge for those who needed her help but couldn't afford to pay. Some who had no money paid Julina with a big sack of potatoes, a bushel of apples, or a few dozen eggs.

Joseph Fielding learned to work hard. At his mother's side, Joseph Fielding learned to bake bread, make pies, and piece together quilts. As they sat together at the kitchen table, peeling peaches or snapping beans, Julina would sing songs to make the time pass more quickly. Whether they were working, singing, or sharing stories, Joseph Fielding loved to be with his mother.

His work outside on the farm was more dangerous than peeling peaches or snapping beans, though. Joseph Fielding once broke his leg after falling off a hay wagon that had been loaded too high. Another time he fell while picking fruit in a tree, and his leg got caught in the fork of two branches. Things got even worse when an angry wasp stung him as he hung, waiting for his father to rescue him.

That wasn't Joseph Fielding's only unpleasant experience with insects. One day while Joseph Fielding and his brother were out herding cows, they got hungry and bought a loaf of bread from a nearby farm woman. But when they sliced the bread, they discovered it was full of flies! They decided they weren't so hungry after all.

The years of hard work at home and on the farm seemed to prepare Joseph Fielding perfectly for his life of service to the Church. He always joked that his first official "church assignment" was when he accompanied his parents to the dedication of the St. George Temple. He was just a babe-in-arms at the time—nine months old.

At the age of twenty-three, Joseph Fielding went out on his own when he was called on a mission to Great Britain. He left not only his parents behind, but a beautiful bride too. Joseph Fielding had met Louie Shurtliff when she came to Salt Lake City to attend school. She was a tall, pretty girl with dark hair and a bright mind. Joseph Fielding said she was the most beautiful girl he had ever seen. It was love at first sight.

They were married in the Salt Lake Temple in 1898, and a year later Joseph Fielding received his mission call. Louie stayed

Joseph Fielding Smith, age twenty-three, as a missionary in Great Britain. Photographer unknown, ca. 1899.

in Utah and taught school while her handsome young husband crossed the ocean to preach the gospel.

The mission was a difficult experience for Joseph Fielding. Many of the people he hoped to teach had heard false and unfair stories about the "Mormons" and refused to listen to his message. Meetings had to be canceled because no one came to listen. Most people slammed their doors in his face. He was unable to baptize a single person while in England. To add to his frustration, he missed his wife. But he wrote home to Louie, "I would rather stay here forever than come home without an honorable record and release."

He received his honorable release two years later, and Joseph Fielding returned home a much stronger Latter-day Saint. He had seen hatred and anger in the eyes of those who rejected him. He now had a greater appreciation for the peace and happiness that come to people who live the gospel. While in England, he had studied the gospel faithfully (he was still a bookworm), and he had learned to defend the truth.

A few months after Joseph Fielding's return in 1901, his father, Joseph F., was sustained as president of the Church. Joseph Fielding worked in the Church Historian's office and helped his father with the huge amount of letter-writing the president had to do. He and his wife Louie were happy to be together again and became the parents of two daughters.

But great sadness came to their home in 1908 when Louie died while expecting their third child. After many sad and lonely months for him and his heartbroken little daughters, Joseph Fielding met and married Ethel G. Reynolds. She was a loving mother to his two little girls, and they accepted her with open arms. Joseph Fielding and Ethel became the parents of nine more children. Theirs was a large and happy family.

Then in 1910, at the age of thirty-three, Joseph Fielding was called to be a new member of the Quorum of the Twelve Apostles. During his travels as an apostle, Joseph Fielding was frequently asked important questions about the gospel. His excellent knowledge of the scriptures enabled him to answer the questions in a way people could easily understand. Some of his teachings were later compiled in *Answers to Gospel Questions* and *Doctrines of Salvation.* He also wrote *Essentials in Church History* and compiled *Teachings of the Prophet Joseph Smith.*

Joseph Fielding especially loved genealogy and Church history. He was a counselor in the presidency of the Salt Lake Temple for sixteen years and was the first editor of the *Utah Genealogical and Historical Magazine,* which started in 1910. He served as Church Historian for forty-nine years—from 1921 to 1970.

As an apostle, Joseph Fielding toured the Church missions in Europe. As the political situation became more dangerous in that area because of World War II, he arranged for all missionaries in Europe to return to the United States. They were sent safely across the Atlantic Ocean on twenty-three ships and assigned to other missions.

To those who didn't know him very well, Joseph Fielding seemed to be a serious, stern man who rarely joked or laughed. But to his family, he was a warm, loving father and husband who wanted more than anything to make his family happy. His second wife, Ethel, once said:

> He is the man that lulls to sleep the fretful child, who tells bedtime stories to the little ones, who is never too tired or too busy to sit up late at night or get up early in the morning to help the older children solve perplexing school problems. He gladly welcomes the young people to his home

Joseph Fielding Smith (#17), age thirty seven, in Deseret Gymnasium, with other members of the gym. Photograph by Johnson Company of Salt Lake City, November 1913.

and is never happier than when discussing with them topics of the day—sports or whatever interests them most.

At home Joseph Fielding often put on an apron and spent almost an entire day baking pies! What a treat for his children to be sent off in every direction gathering ingredients for a whole kitchen full of delicious pies: apple, pumpkin, peach, cherry, and mincemeat!

When one of his children did something wrong, he was too tender-hearted to spank them. After talking to them about their misdeed, he would put his hands on their shoulders, look them in the eyes, and say, "I wish my kiddies would be good."

Joseph Fielding loved sports. He was an excellent swimmer and handball player and could win a game of handball with any of his five sons with one hand behind his back. He loved to watch sporting activities, especially if his children or grand-children were participating.

Even after becoming a grandfather, Joseph Fielding was very adventurous. He loved flying in jet airplanes. He sometimes flew with a friend in the National Guard. Once Joseph Fielding was in the air, he was often allowed to take over the controls. One day as he was flying over Salt Lake City, a friend came looking for him in his office. His secretary told the man that if he looked out the window he could see Joseph Fielding. As the friend leaned out the window, he could see Brother Smith's plane doing loops and dives in the air. This hobby continued until he was in his nineties.

In 1937, Joseph Fielding had the sad experience again of losing his wife. Ethel, who had been such a wonderful mother to their eleven children, died after being sick for a long time.

Again Joseph Fielding needed a companion, and he married Jessie Ella Evans, a well-known singer. "Aunt Jessie," as she was called by the Smith family, was a happy, fun-loving woman who brought much happiness to Joseph Fielding and his family. She enjoyed traveling with him and often shared her musical talent by singing in Church meetings. Many times she and Joseph Fielding sang duets.

Aunt Jessie often did things that surprised those who ex-pected a more serious woman to be married to an apostle. Once the couple were standing on the sidewalk waiting for a friend to pick them up in a car. She saw their friend drive by without seeing them, so she quickly put her fingers in her mouth and whistled very loud! The driver heard her signal and came back to get them.

Joseph Fielding Smith became president of the Church when he was ninety-three years old. Many people whispered to each other that he was much too old to lead the Church. But the

Joseph Fielding Smith loved airplanes and flying. Here, he is seated in the cockpit of a Utah Air National Guard jet airplane. Photographer unknown.

Lord wanted Joseph Fielding to be the prophet and blessed him with good health and energy. During the two-and-one-half years he served as president, he held special conferences in California, Arizona, Idaho, Missouri, and Hawaii. He returned to the British Isles for an area conference, where he had served as a missionary seventy years earlier.

During his presidency, Joseph Fielding set aside Monday as family home evening night. Above all, he continued to bear his strong testimony that the gospel is true. He said:

> If this Church were the work of man, it would fail, but it is the work of the Lord, and he does not fail. If we keep the commandments and are valiant in the testimony of Jesus, the Lord will guide and direct us and his Church in the paths of righteousness.

President Smith died July 2, 1972, while peacefully sitting in his favorite chair at a daughter's home. He was nearly ninety-six years old.

Joseph Fielding Smith loved children and would often be seen hugging them. Photographer unknown.

Harold B. Lee

A Bishop's Son Who Helped the Poor

On March 28, 1899, Clifton, Idaho, had eighty-two families, one general store, and a blacksmith shop. It also had a sheriff, a school teacher, two carpet weavers, a one-room Church meetinghouse, a swimming hole called Dudley's Pond, and lots of cows, chickens, and sheep. Everyone had to pick up their mail at the home of Harriett Henderson since the post office had burned down a few years earlier.

A narrow road called "the string" ran through Clifton and then wandered off into the countryside. That road was either dusty, muddy, or snow-covered, depending on the time of year.

On this particular day in March "out on the string, two miles north of the store," there was a small cabin where Clifton's most famous citizen had just been born: Harold Bingham Lee. Of course, nobody knew Harold was Clifton's most famous citizen—that would happen much later. If they had known he was going to become the president of the Church, for instance, they may have given the road some fancy, important name. But as it was, his birthplace was simply "out on the string, two miles north of the store."

The first thing people noticed about little Harold B. Lee was his beautiful, wavy brown hair. His mother liked it so much,

Harold B. Lee, age five, with his older brother, Perry, to the right. Photographer unknown, ca. 1904.

in fact, she let it grow out long and trained it into ringlets that fell below his shoulders. Well, this was fine as long as the neighborhood ladies were the only ones to see him. They thought he was absolutely darling dressed up in the frilly suits his mother sewed for him, complete with ruffles and lace-trimmed sleeves. His ringlets provided the crowning touch, they thought.

Unfortunately, when Harold was old enough to go to school, his friends didn't think he was so cute. Instead of admiring his ringlets, they laughed and pulled on them! A few skinned knuckles and black eyes later, Harold decided he had had enough. He raced home, went straight for the kitchen knife, and sawed off one of the ringlets. This, of course, spoiled the whole effect, and his heart-broken mother was forced to cut off the remaining curls. Harold's grandfather, Deputy Warden Bingham of the Idaho State Prison, convinced one of the prisoners to braid the long curls into two watch chains. Harold's mother kept them among her treasures.

Harold's parents, Samuel Marion Lee, Jr., and Louisa Bingham, reared six children on their small farm nestled at the foot of the Wasatch Mountains in Cache Valley. Harold was their second child.

Margaret Lee, Harold's grandmother, had given birth to eleven babies, all of whom died shortly after birth. Then her twelfth child Samuel (Harold's father) was born, but she herself died, leaving him to be reared by his grandparents. He weighed only 3 1/2 pounds and was so small that a wedding ring could be slipped over his arm. After his marriage to Louisa Bingham, Samuel became a school teacher, farmer, store manager, and bishop of the Clifton Ward. He was known as "one of the warmest, friendliest men" in town.

Louisa had grown up having to do household chores at an early age, including cooking, sewing, and laundry, since her mother was often sick and unable to care for the family. Louisa's ability to run a household came in handy as she reared her own children. She was an excellent homemaker, and the home often smelled of homemade bread and pies. Sometimes the smells were almost unbearably wonderful as the children lay in bed at night. Often their father would finally carry them down to the kitchen for a thick slice of bread smothered in butter and honey.

Farm life taught Harold to work hard and use his time wisely. These lessons were important for a boy who would spend most of his life doing the Lord's work. After a day of milking cows, planting crops, caring for the garden, and mending fences, Harold was ready for bed at night. If he ever considered wandering off to play without doing his chores first, Harold knew his mother would quickly change his mind with a few switches from "the little green willow."

Sunday brought a day of rest for the family and a chance to attend Church meetings. Life on the farm provided tempting distractions for the children on this day of worship. One teacher, for instance, emphasized the importance of the Sabbath by reminding some of Harold's playmates that they "should attend Sunday School instead of riding their horses on the range." But Harold faithfully attended all his meetings.

Along with the other church members, the Lee family donated nickels, butter, and eggs to buy Church materials and keep up the meetinghouse. When Harold was a deacon, part of his responsibility was to help take care of the church house. He washed the chimney, filled coal-oil lamps, swept the floor, and chopped wood for the stove.

During the years his father served as bishop of their ward, Harold often helped his father load sacks of grain or bundles of clothing into the back of their pony cart. Then after sunset, so as to protect the privacy of those he would visit, Harold's father would take the load to distribute to the poor and needy in his ward. This made a lasting impression on young Harold, and he would remember his father's kindness many years later when he was called to organize a welfare program for the entire Church.

Harold took piano lessons and played for Church meetings and for the enjoyment of his family and friends. One day when Harold and his brother Perry were in bed with scarlet fever, their father came through the front door, smiling, with two new shiny instruments: a cornet in one hand and a baritone horn in the other. The boys instantly fell in love with their brassy sounds. They practiced faithfully until they became skillful enough to join the Silver Cornet Band of Clifton. They performed in parades and outdoor concerts on special occasions like the Fourth of July.

Harold's life was saved many times by his mother's expert skill as a nurse. She sat by his bedside many a night bringing down the temperature of a fever or tending to his illnesses with homemade remedies. Harold came down with a dangerous case of pneumonia one night, but Louisa seemed to know just what to do:

> She hurried to the back porch and opened a large sack of onions, filled her apron, and went into the kitchen. After slicing a large panful of onions she dumped them into an empty flour sack and covered her son's chest with the wet, juicy sack. Then she prayed and waited for a miracle. By morning his breathing was improved and his life was out of danger. When the family praised Louisa for saving his life, she merely said, "Oh, I didn't save his life. The Lord did. He just expects us to do everything we can do to help."

The hand of the Lord seemed to guide Louisa at other times when she saved Harold's life through her quick thinking. She once pushed him away from the open front door of their house during a thunderstorm just seconds before a lightning bolt came down the chimney of the kitchen stove, jumped out through the open doorway, and split a huge gash in a large tree in their front yard.

Another time a huge tub of poisonous lye (used for making soap) slipped out of Louisa's hands and came down off a shelf on top of Harold—covering his head, face, and arms. Quick as could be, Louisa kicked off the lid of a jar of pickled beets, dipped out the reddened pickle vinegar with her cupped hands, and poured it over her son's skin to stop the lye from causing dangerous burns. The liquid soothed the pain, and Harold recovered completely with no scars.

Harold and his brothers and sisters rode to school in a two-wheeled cart pulled by a pony driven by their mother. Harold loved school and did well in his studies. After completing at age thirteen the elementary grades at the local Clifton School, he attended the Oneida Stake Academy in Preston, fifteen miles from home, for his high school education. One of his classmates was another future prophet—Ezra Taft Benson.

Harold decided early on he wanted to become a teacher. He got along well with people and had an outgoing personality. He went to the Albion State Normal School to earn his teaching certificate and passed the final exams with high scores. He must have studied hard, though. He lost twenty pounds while preparing for the tests!

Harold was only seventeen years old when he got his first teaching job at the Silver Star School, a one-room school near Weston, Idaho. Some of the students were older than he was. The school had a pot-bellied stove in the middle of the room to keep them warm. This stove had a long pipe that had a habit

Harold B. Lee taught at this one-room school house, Silver Star School. Photographer unknown.

of falling down, scattering black soot everywhere, and filling the room with smoke.

A year later Harold was hired as the principal of the nearby Oxford School. Some of his students were rather rough and mischievous, and Harold had his hands full keeping the classroom in order. They once hid his horse while he was visiting with someone, and he had to walk several miles home. But he soon made friends with the students by playing basketball with them during their lunch break.

After teaching school for four years, Harold was called by President Heber J. Grant to the Western States Mission, headquartered in Denver, Colorado. This experience was crucial for the future prophet. Elder Lee improved his speaking ability, learned to use the scriptures, blessed the sick, comforted those who were sad and lonely, and taught the gospel. He baptized forty-five converts. Harold also learned to accept disappointment when things didn't go the way he wanted them to. They often went for days without being invited into someone's home to share the gospel.

Harold and a missionary companion named Willis J. Woodbury used an unusual approach with some of the people they taught. Elder Woodbury carried a cello with him when they went out knocking on doors. When they were invited into a home, Elder Woodbury would play the cello while Elder Lee accompanied on the piano. They played sacred music, which made their listeners better prepared to listen to a gospel message.

Harold enjoyed missionary work so much, in fact, he was disappointed when the time came for him to be released after serving for more than two years. That disappointment didn't last long, however, once he got home. After a short stay in Clifton with his family, Harold moved to Salt Lake City with the idea of dating Fern Tanner, a young lady he had met in the mission

Harold B. Lee, age twenty-one, while he was principal at Oxford School. Photographer unknown, 1920.

field. They fell in love and were married in the Salt Lake Temple in 1923. They became the parents of two daughters: Maurine and Helen.

During the early years of their marriage, Harold completed his education and worked hard to support his little family. He was the principal first of the Whittier School and then of the Woodrow Wilson School in the Granite School District. He also sold meat for Swift and Company, inspected Salt Lake City street department equipment, and was a watchman for Union Pacific Railroad Company.

Harold loved his wife and two children very much. Together they enjoyed hiking in the canyons, going out to a local drive-in for ice cold root beer, and cooking hamburgers at home out on the back patio. Harold especially loved playing the piano for his family. His daughters' absolute favorite piece was called the "Midnight Fire Alarm." Helen described the scene at home when he started playing this lively tune:

> Maurine and I would dance and prance around the room as Daddy was playing this exciting, loud music. He played with such enthusiasm that the entire house seemed to vibrate, and we loved it! Once he finished a real work out performance with such flourish that he could see he had thoroughly delighted us, as well as some of our little friends who were with us. He felt especially pleased when he overheard Maurine's friend say "Gee, that was really good, wasn't it?" Maurine answered, "Uh, huh, and the best part about it is watching the piano shake!"

Helen also tells of how he could settle an argument at the dinner table and still leave her and her sister feeling good about themselves:

> Daddy used to sit at the end of the table and Mother sat on his right. My sister and I would contend about who was going to sit on his left. Both of us wanted the honor of sitting closest to Daddy, on the other side of him. Maurine had chosen first to sit by Daddy at this particular meal and I said, "Oh, but you sat there last time and now it's my turn." She countered, "But I chose first."
> Then the master teacher resolved the argument. Turning

to me he said, "Now Helen, I need you to sit across the table from me for a very special reason. You know I have a terrible time with this soup and sometimes I spill it on my tie or on my shirt. Now, if you sit right there across from me you can watch Daddy and make certain I don't spill anything on this nice new tie." After that I was perfectly happy with my place of honor, sitting facing him, contented with the responsibility of watching him and making certain he didn't get any spots on his tie.

Harold had two very sad experiences with his family. In 1962, his wife, Fern, died. They had been married thirty-nine years, and her death brought him much sorrow and loneliness. He was grateful to find another companion, Freda Joan Jensen, whom he married in 1963.

The second sad experience came just three years later, in 1966, when his daughter Maurine died unexpectedly. He was deeply saddened by this experience and felt especially sorry for her husband and the four small children she left behind. After these experiences he told a group:

> Death of a loved one is the most severe test that you will ever face, and if you can rise above your griefs and if you will trust in God, then you will be able to surmount any other difficulty with which you may be faced.

From 1930 to 1937, Harold served as president of the Pioneer Stake in Salt Lake City. He was thirty-one years old when he was called to this position, making him the youngest stake president in the Church at that time.

The first Christmas after Harold had been made a stake president, he learned a great lesson. He found a family nearby who had no Christmas gifts because their father was out of work. President Lee felt very sad about this. That night he knelt down and prayed to his Heavenly Father:

God grant that I will never let another year pass but that I, as a leader, will truly know my people. I will know their needs, I will be conscious of those who most need my leadership, and I will help them.

Remembering the example of his father in Clifton, Idaho, Harold B. Lee immediately went to work setting up a program in his stake to help the needy. He called together all the ward and stake leaders to set up a "stake welfare program." Members of the stake donated money, fruit bottles, clothing, and furniture to be stored and distributed to those found in need by their ward bishops.

Stake members who were without jobs could work by sewing, repairing furniture, working on Church construction projects, or by helping farmers with their crops. They were then paid by receiving a portion of the crop in return or by receiving goods from the stake warehouse.

Under President Lee's direction, a stake gymnasium was built at great sacrifice to provide the members with a place to enjoy themselves and socialize with other Church members. Warmth and food was available to anyone who came. Many meals were provided for families who would otherwise have gone hungry.

The plan worked beautifully. Church president Heber J. Grant soon called Harold B. Lee into his office and asked him to be the director of a welfare program for the whole Church. President Lee was very humbled and a bit scared to receive such an important assignment. He was only thirty-six years old and knew he would need help from his Heavenly Father to accomplish this assignment. "With his help I cannot fail," he later said. "Without it I cannot succeed."

On April 10, 1941, when Harold B. Lee was forty-two years old, he was called to be a member of the Quorum of the Twelve

As stake president, Harold B. Lee set up a program in the Pioneer Stake to assist the needy. That included the establishment of this storehouse. Photographer unknown.

Apostles. He was at least twenty years younger than any other member of the quorum and sometimes felt like "a seedling among redwood trees."

Elder Lee's talents and abilities made it possible for him to serve the Church in many different ways. His love of music helped him in his assignment as chairman of the Church Music Committee. He loved children and was the advisor to the Primary general board. He was a good speaker and gave a series of Sunday evening radio talks called "Youth and the Church." He loved people of all nationalities and bore his strong testimony of the gospel in countries all over the world.

Elder Lee served as an apostle for thirty-one years before becoming president of the Church on July 7, 1972, after the death of President Joseph Fielding Smith. In a special quiet, holy room of the Salt Lake Temple, each member of the Quorum of the Twelve Apostles stood in a circle around Harold Bingham Lee, laid their hands on his head, and ordained him to this "high and incomparable calling."

Now, more than ever before, President Lee needed the help of the Lord. He told a story in the April 1973 general conference of how close his Heavenly Father was to him during this time:

> I was suffering from an ulcer condition that was becoming worse and worse. We had been touring a mission; my wife, Joan, and I were impressed the next morning that we should get home as quickly as possible, although we had planned to stay for some other meetings.
>
> On the way home, we were sitting in the front section of the airplane. At a certain point in the trip, someone laid his hand upon my head. I looked up; I could see no one. That happened again before we arrived home. What it was, by what means or medium I may never know, except I knew that I was receiving a blessing that I came a few hours later to know I needed most desperately.
>
> As soon as we arrived home, my wife called the doctor. He called me to come to the telephone and he asked me how I was; and I said, 'Well, I am very tired. I think I will be all right.'
>
> But soon after, there came massive bleeding which, had it occurred in flight, I wouldn't be here today talking about it. I know that there are powers divine that reach out when all other help is not available. Yes, I know that there are such powers.

Harold B. Lee, about age fifty-eight, at the dedication of the Timpa-nogas Region Bishops' Storehouse. With him, from left to right, are Mark B. Garff; Clifford E. Young; J. Reuben Clark, Jr., Second Coun-selor in the First Presidency; and Phil W. Jensen. Photographer un-known, 1957.

Harold Bingham Lee served as prophet, seer, and revelator of the Church from July 7, 1972 to December 26, 1973 — seventeen months. He was seventy-four years old when he died in a Salt Lake hospital from heart and lung failure.

Dr. Norman Vincent Peale, a famous author and pastor of a church in New York City, said after President Lee's death: "I admired him tremendously. He was one of the most enlightened and creative religious leaders in the world. A giant has fallen."

President Lee's life had traveled a long road to the highest calling in The Church of Jesus Christ of Latter-day Saints—a life that began in Clifton, Idaho, "out on the string, two miles north of the store."

Harold B. Lee, about age seventy-two. Photograph by Merrett Smith, ca. 1971.

Spencer W. Kimball

A Life Like His Shoes, to Be Worn Out in Service

When three-year-old Spencer Woolley Kimball climbed on board a train in Salt Lake City with his family in 1898, he hadn't the faintest idea where they were going. He kept hearing everyone talk in soft voices about "Arizona," but he didn't know where it was or how long they would stay. He noticed everyone seemed very sad. Spencer wondered if someone had died.

His parents, Andrew and Olive Woolley Kimball, had received a call from President Wilford Woodruff, a prophet of God, to move to the Gila (pronounced *Hee la*) Valley in the desert of southeastern Arizona where Spencer's father would serve as stake president.

Friends who returned to Salt Lake City from this place in Arizona described it as "a desert wasteland," "hot and dry," and "infested with spiders and flies." One settler said of the plants and animals there: "If you touch it, it stings you; if you pet it, it bites you; and if you eat it, it kills you!"

Arizona didn't sound very inviting to the Kimball family, but they faithfully accepted the call because they believed it came from the Lord. In the rain, Spencer huddled under an umbrella

Andrew and Olive Kimball family, 1897. Older children from left to right are Ruth, Gordon, Clare, and Delbert. The infants are Alice (left) and Spencer (right). Photographer unknown.

while his mother tearfully kissed her friends good-bye, saving the last hug for Spencer's Grandmother Woolley just before the train pulled away.

Spencer would soon forget Salt Lake City. The small town of Thatcher, Arizona, would quickly become his home. And he would love it.

Spencer Woolley Kimball was born March 28, 1895, in a small brick home in Salt Lake City. Upon hearing the news of his arrival, Clare, his ten-year-old sister, had a crying spell because she had been hoping for a little sister. Spencer was the sixth of the eleven Kimball children.

It soon became clear that he would be very bright, happy, and . . . short. "I sit tall but stand short," he often said. Spencer inherited his stature from his mother, Olive, who stood just five feet tall. She was a very kind and spiritual woman with a round pretty face, blue eyes, and reddish hair. Spencer's father, Andrew, was six feet tall and slender. Spencer got his dark eyes and black hair from his father.

What Spencer lacked in height, he made up in energy and physical strength. "I could outwrestle almost any boy that was near my size," he once said. "I was tough and strong . . . and pretty husky."

Like most children, Spencer loved to romp and play and tease. His brothers called him a "busy-body." At the Thatcher school he attended after their move to Arizona, the fifteen minutes of recess were precious. Marbles, pop-the-whip, pom-pom-pull-away, and leap frog were all favorite games. Spencer once chased a girl around the school yard with a fat caterpillar just to hear her scream. Another time he doused Ella Tyler with a bucket of water. She later said, "The only reason Spencer Kimball lived to become a General Authority is that I am a slow runner."

Spencer was a happy boy, but his laughter in the classroom often got him into trouble. More than once he had to come up and sit by the teacher's desk because he and Agnes Chlarson couldn't stop giggling. "I got serious finally," he remembered.

Spencer's father made sure his children had little time for mischief. When Spencer wasn't in school, he was busy on the family farm pitching hay, mixing paint, beating carpets, and trimming trees. There was no loafing. Spencer always had weeds to chop, a garden to tend, and fences to build. By the end of the day, Spencer was so tired he often fell asleep at the supper table.

Along with the day's work, Spencer always found ways to
amuse himself. When they butchered a hog for the family's
supply of meat, Spencer asked for the pig's bladder. He cleaned
the fat off, washed it, and blew it up into a ball. To fight boredom
as he pumped water or milked cows, Spencer would say his
ABCs forward and backward, recite the Articles of Faith, and
memorize scriptures. One day Spencer's father overheard him
singing church hymns while milking. He said to a neighbor who
was standing nearby, "That Spencer is a good boy. I have dedicated him to the Lord, and someday he will become a mighty
man in the Church."

Spencer loved the gospel and enjoyed going to Primary, which
was then held during the week in the afternoon. His brothers,
however, sometimes thought he dashed off to the cool chapel
just to get out of hauling hay in the sweltering Arizona heat.

Thatcher was a farming community and had a population
of eight hundred people, including a few odd characters. There
was the mailman, for instance, with one ear missing. And Ernest
Jones' horse, which Spencer called Napoleon Bonaparte because
he had such "bony parts." Then there was the neighbor whose
hair was so long and bushy that each time the Kimball boys
lost a pair of scissors, or a tool, a pair of shoes, or one of the
cows, they would joke: "Maybe it is lost in Brother Sessions'
hair!"

On Spencer's eighth birthday, his father baptized him in a
big metal vat that they sometimes used as a bathtub. But four
years later someone suggested the baptism might not be quite
right because his father wasn't standing in the water with him.
So Spencer was baptized again in the Union Canal where the
boys often went swimming.

Spencer's father was often away from home working at various occupations: selling Bibles, insurance, suits, and medicines;

serving in the state legislature; and representing the railroad company. Much of Spencer's world thus revolved around his dear mother. He wrote:

> My mother was faultless. She was a saint. Who could even imagine one virtue that she did not possess? She seemed especially angelic when the light shined through her light red hair and made a halo. I liked being with my Ma.

Olive Kimball taught her children religion. As she and the children sat on the fourth row of the Thatcher meetinghouse, Spencer often laid his head in his mother's lap. The Kimball family always knelt for prayer before meals, their chairs turned back from the table and their dinner plates upside down. Spencer said his prayers each night at his mother's knees.

Spencer's happy boyhood seemed to come to an end when he was eleven years old. That was when his mother died. She had been very ill while expecting her twelfth child and died in a hospital in Salt Lake City. Their bishop in Thatcher called the Kimball children out of school and told them as gently as he could, "Your Ma is dead." The terrible news hit Spencer like a thunderbolt. He ran outside to be alone and cried until he thought his heart would burst.

Five days later Spencer's father returned to Thatcher, bringing Olive's body in a coffin. After the sad funeral, sixty-five carriages followed her coffin to the cemetery. Spencer was heartbroken. "Life couldn't go on for us," he cried.

But the Lord blessed young Spencer and helped him find the courage to live a good life without his mother near. He watched while other boys stole watermelons from a neighbor's patch, but he refused to participate. He thought it was unfair to the farmers who had worked so hard to grow the melons. Other times, his friends would kill birds while testing their slingshots.

Spencer remembered a song he had learned in Sunday School, "Don't Kill the Little Birds." His parents had taught him to treat all animals kindly.

About the time Spencer was ordained a deacon, he heard Brigham Young's daughter Susa Young Gates speak in stake conference. When she asked who in the congregation had read the whole Bible, Spencer saw only a few hands go up. He decided to accept the challenge. As soon as he got home, he lit the coal-oil lamp, went up into the attic, and started to read from the book of Genesis. A year later, Spencer had finished reading through the whole Bible. Although he did not understand everything he had read, he was proud of accomplishing this goal.

After graduating from grade school, Spencer attended the Gila Academy, which was like a combined junior high and high school. He was a good student, had lots of friends, and served as class president each year. He especially loved playing basketball. In fact, he loved playing it so much that he was often scolded for staying after school too long to play ball. After all, the neighbors were waiting to buy milk from the cows he was late in milking.

At Spencer's high school graduation, his father announced to the audience that Spencer would be going on a mission for the Church at the end of the summer! This was a complete surprise to him, but Spencer was happy and willing to go. Spencer would have to pay most of his own way, so he needed to earn some money. The first thing he did was sell his spirited black horse. That brought enough money to keep him in the mission field six months.

Spencer then got a summer job working at a dairy in a nearby town for $62.50 a month plus his meals and a bed to sleep in at night. He fed and milked cows, washed bottles, cared for the calves, and cleaned up the barn. Sometimes his fingers would

Gila Academy basketball team, 1912–13. Spencer W. Kimball, about age seventeen, is standing far right. Photographer unknown.

be so dry and tender from the work that they would swell up, crack, and bleed. But even so, Spencer remained a faithful, dependable worker. That pleased his boss at the dairy, and at the end of the summer, when it was time for Spencer to leave on his mission, his boss held a farewell party for him and presented him with a beautiful gold watch.

Spencer was nineteen years old when he left to serve a mis-

Spencer W. Kimball, about age twenty, as a missionary in the Central States Mission. Photographer unknown, 1915.

sion in the Central States. He learned quickly that missionary work would not be easy. Shortly after he arrived in Missouri, Spencer and his companion were assigned to start knocking on doors in the country outside Jefferson City. As it got later in the evening, they began asking for a place to sleep that night. They were turned down time after time. Finally, near midnight, a grouchy man invited them in and said that they could sleep on an extra bed he had up in his attic. The next morning, Spencer and his companion found themselves bitten all over by bed bugs. Their bed was spotted with blood from the bites. Still, they were grateful for the man's hospitality.

Spencer's father knew he would have some difficult days, so he wrote words of encouragement:

> You will make good, Spencer. You are small in stature— so was your sweet mother—but big natured and whole souled. Your hard experiences will enable you to know just a little of what it costs to be a Latter-day Saint and something of what your father and grandfather waded through. Keep up a good courageous spirit, but don't get to think it is too much for you to bear. It will all come out well and you will have something to tell your posterity.

Soon after Spencer returned home from his mission in 1917, he met and married Camilla Eyring, an attractive new teacher at the Gila Academy. On their wedding day, November 16, 1917, Spencer was hurrying to get ready for the wedding ceremony. He was so excited that he undressed and stepped into the metal tub before he realized he had forgotten to fill it with water! He called for his stepmother, Josie, to bring him buckets of hot water and hand them to him around the partially open door.

During the first year of their marriage, Camilla continued to teach at the academy, and Spencer worked on farms in the

Spencer W. and Camilla Eyring Kimball shortly after their marriage. Photographer unknown, ca. 1917.

area and then got a job at a local bank. With some of the first money he earned, Spencer bought Camilla a wedding ring for seven dollars.

After saving every penny they could for seven months, Spencer and Camilla had enough money to travel to Salt Lake City to be sealed in the temple for time and all eternity.

They became the parents of four children, Spencer LeVan, Olive Beth, Andrew Eyring, and Edward Lawrence. These years were busy ones for Spencer and Camilla. They devoted much of their time to rearing their family, contributing to the community, and serving in the Church.

Camilla helped to organize the PTA at their children's school and to get a public library started in Safford, the neighboring town to which they had moved. She kept a clean house, baked cinnamon rolls and bread, bottled fruit, and scrubbed clothes on a washboard until sweat dripped off her nose. She taught her children to love books and work hard on their school studies. All four of the Kimball children were excellent students, and each later graduated with college degrees.

Spencer continued working as a bank teller. He earned extra money playing piano in a dance band and serving as a stake clerk for the Church—which at that time was a paid part-time job. He and a partner later went into business together selling insurance and real estate. Their advertising sign read: "See us before you buy, burn, or die."

A new stake, Mt. Graham, was created in 1938, and Spencer Kimball was called to be the stake president. After accepting the calling, he made a point of visiting and apologizing to those he had had disagreements with so he could serve "with a free conscience."

Spencer drove great distances throughout his stake visiting the sick, performing weddings, giving counsel to those who were troubled, and giving talks. The Saints loved him. Sometimes he was so busy that news had trouble catching up with him. On one such trip, he had been invited to speak at a funeral and was shocked to see the man whose funeral he thought it was walk in and take a seat on the front row. It turned out that the funeral was for the man's brother.

In 1942, Spencer and Camilla built their "dream house" and celebrated their twenty-fifth wedding anniversary. They invited over six hundred friends to come to their home and help

celebrate with food and visiting. They were very happy and felt
sure they would stay in their new home the rest of their lives.
They assumed they would have a quiet, relaxing retirement years
down the road.

But big changes were in store for Spencer and Camilla Kimball. In July 1943, Spencer received a phone call from Salt Lake
City saying he had been chosen as a member of the Quorum
of the Twelve Apostles. Spencer was so shocked he slowly sat
down, missed a chair, and sank to the floor!

This calling would mean a great sacrifice for the Kimball
family. They would have to give up their business in Arizona,
which Spencer had worked for many years to build; they would
have to move to Salt Lake City, leaving behind lifelong friends;
and he would be given Church responsibilities he didn't feel
capable of performing. Spencer began to weep and could not
stop. Camilla took him in her arms and comforted him. "You
can do it," she reassured. "You can do anything the Lord asks
of you."

Spencer prayed almost constantly for six days and nights for
the Lord to give him the strength and courage he needed to meet
this new challenge. While visiting his son in Colorado soon after
his call, Spencer went hiking in the mountains early one morning. He struggled, agonizing, praying for confirmation that the
call he had received was from God. Finally the reassurance came.
It came like the calm of the dying wind, the quieting wave after
a storm is over. That morning his soul felt a beautiful peace
that brought him closer to his Heavenly Father than ever before
in his life. At forty-eight years of age, Spencer started a new life.
He was sustained as an apostle at the October 1943 Semiannual
General Conference.

Spencer worked hard in service to the Lord. He traveled thousands of miles to visit the Saints, call new leaders, and speak

at firesides. While attending stake conferences, Spencer usually stayed in stake leaders' homes. He would play the piano for the children, singing Primary songs for them. "They'll forget my sermons," he said, "but they'll never forget our singing." He also helped with the chores. If a stake president's farm had cows he did a share of the milking.

After serving as an apostle several years, Spencer was visited by a group of Primary children. When the teacher asked the class if they knew who this man was, there was silence. Finally one small boy looked at the apostle, trying to remember, and answered, "I know I've seen that mug somewhere!" It was a "mug" that millions of Saints all over the world would learn to love.

Spencer had a special love for the Lamanite people and visited the reservations, meeting members, teaching and encouraging them to live the gospel, and blessing the sick. He helped the Indian people get better schools and better roads in order to solve some of their problems. He helped start the Indian Student Placement Program, which made it possible for thousands of children each year to live in Latter-day Saint homes while attending school.

Spencer accomplished so much during those years, it's hard to believe that he was suffering from many serious health problems. As a boy, he suffered from typhoid and Bell's palsy, which paralyzed his face. As a young adult he had smallpox. He had painful boils over much of his body for long periods of time. He had heart attacks. He had to have most of his vocal cords removed in 1957 because of cancer and had to learn to speak all over again. In 1972, he had open-heart surgery, and in 1979 and 1981 he had brain surgery. When someone once called him a "modern miracle," he replied, "Haven't you read in the scrip-

Spencer W. Kimball visits Indians on a reservation in the Southwest. As an apostle, he worked with Indians to improve their education and life-style. Photographer unknown.

tures that men will be strengthened even to the renewing of their bodies, if they are doing the work of the Lord?"

Spencer Woolley Kimball became president of The Church of Jesus Christ of Latter-day Saints on December 30, 1973, upon the death of President Harold B. Lee. Spencer had been an apostle for thirty years and was seventy-eight years old. Most people knew he had many health problems, and they did not expect him to live much longer. They thought that President Kimball wouldn't have the energy to accomplish much and that his administration would be short. One little boy, brought into his office to shake his hand, said "I wanted to see you before you died."

But President Kimball served as prophet, seer, and revelator for nearly twelve years, and that time was full of exciting changes and accomplishments. He announced the building of dozens of new smaller temples all over the world. He held area conferences in many countries and inspired the Saints with his messages. In 1978, after much prayer and pleading with the Lord in the Salt Lake Temple, President Kimball received a revelation that the priesthood would now be available to every worthy male member of the Church, regardless of race or color. This was perhaps the most exciting event of all.

"Lengthen your stride" and "Do it" became President Kimball's advice to the Saints as he encouraged them to do more missionary work, attend the temple more often, and perform their Church callings more diligently.

President Kimball continued to be considerate and thoughtful of those around him. He and Camilla once had a buffet meal in their home after general conference. Because of threats that had been made against the Church and the president, the city had posted a policeman outside their home for safety. During the meal, Spencer filled a plate with food and slipped out of the house to take it to the policeman on duty in the patrol car.

Another time, on New Year's Day, four teenage boys rang the doorbell at President Kimball's home. He invited them in, chatted pleasantly, and posed with them for pictures. He found out that they hadn't eaten, so Camilla fixed them each a plate of food. When they left, a member of his family asked, "Was all of that really necessary?" President Kimball replied, "I belong to all the people, not just my family."

President Kimball was a faithful journal keeper most of his life. He had a whole shelf of binders filled with typewritten entries. His journal included photographs and pictures cut out of magazines and newspapers. He also wrote books. His book *The Miracle of Forgiveness* has helped thousands of people understand the importance of repentance.

President Kimball was very sick the last few years of his life but continued to attend weekly meetings in the Salt Lake Temple and discuss Church business with his counselors in the First Presidency. As his life came to a close, there was hardly anything short about Spencer W. Kimball, except his height. His life was long, his list of accomplishments in the Church was long, and the impact he had on the lives of the Saints of his day would last forever.

President Kimball died on November 5, 1985, at the age of ninety. He once said, "My life is like my shoes, to be worn out in service." When he died, it was true that his shoes were well-worn and his life was well-lived in the service of God and his fellow men.

Spencer W. Kimball, about age eighty-six. President Kimball loved reading the scriptures whenever he could. Photograph by Eldon Linschoten, 1981.

Ezra Taft Benson

A Scout Who Served God and His Country

It was 1918, and a large crowd filled the Tabernacle in Logan, Utah. The benches on the main floor overflowed with over a hundred young Boy Scouts, all dressed in crisp uniforms dotted with the merit badges they had worked hard to earn. Each Scout had a yellow kerchief tied smartly around his neck. The balcony seats and window sills were packed with anxious parents and friends. But this was neither a court of honor nor a Scout jamboree. It was a boys' choir contest. Each member of the audience was pulling for their ward scout troop to bring home the honor of best young men's choir in the Cache Valley region.

At the start of the competition, lots were drawn for placement on the program, and the honor of singing last fell to the troop from Whitney, Idaho. This group of twenty-four lively young boys had a special reason for wanting to win: Ezra Taft Benson, their assistant Scoutmaster and choir director, had promised to take them on a thirty-five-mile hike from Cache Valley across the mountains to Bear Lake . . . if they came out on top.

When their turn on the program finally came, the boys from Whitney marched confidently up the aisle as the pianist played "Stars and Stripes Forever." Once in place, the eyes of every boy focused on Brother Benson, who had squeezed between two benches to direct the performance. The scouts sang their hearts out and soon heard their troop's name called out as the first place winner.

In an instant, the happy boys crowded around Brother Benson to remind him of the hike he had promised them. Of course he would take them. With approval from the parents, a prehike planning meeting was held. Food, camping gear, and clothing were planned, and the dates for the hike were set. Then one twelve-year-old Scout raised his hand: "Mr. Scoutmaster, I'd like to make a motion. Just to make it easier, we should all clip our hair off so we will not be bothered with combs and brushes on the trip." Everyone agreed, laughing to think what they all would look like with shaved heads.

Just before the hike, the troop paid a visit to the barber shop. When Brother Benson sat in the chair to get a trim, the barber spoke up. "If you'll let me shave your head, I'll cut the hair of the rest of your boys for nothing." The boys roared their approval. Brother Benson grinned and finally agreed.

Two days later, a bald Scoutmaster, with his bald assistants, led twenty-four hairless Scouts on an unforgettable ten-day hike to Bear Lake. The trip was glorious, filled with fishing, camping, hiking, swimming, and brotherhood.

Who could forget a Scouting experience like that! Certainly not Ezra Taft Benson. It brought together many things Ezra loved: the Church, young people, Scouting, the singing of patriotic music, the outdoors, and good clean fun. It remained one of Ezra's happiest leadership memories. The experience also taught Ezra that the Lord had blessed him with a special ability to inspire others to try harder, to reach higher, and to be their best. A future leader for the United States government and the Lord's church was in the making.

Ezra Taft Benson was born August 4, 1899, in the small Mormon settlement of Whitney, Idaho. He was the first of eleven children born to George T. Benson, Jr., and Sarah Dunkley. Ezra's birth was a frightening experience. The doctor was unable to get the eleven-pound baby boy to breathe. He set the baby on the bed and announced sadly, "There's no hope for this child to live, but I believe we can save the mother." While the doctor worked to help the mother, Ezra's two grandmothers fell to their knees and asked the Lord to help them save their precious grandson.

They quickly got two pans of water, one cool and one warm, and began dipping the baby first in one pan and then in the other until finally he let out a loud cry. The women wept for joy when they were sure that the baby would live and that his mother was also out of danger.

Ezra, or "T" as he was called in his youth, was proud of his ancestors. Some of his forefathers had fought in the American Revolution. His great-grandfather Ezra Taft Benson, for whom he was named, was an apostle and a close and trusted friend of Joseph Smith and Brigham Young. Ezra's grandparents, equally faithful, had been among the first settlers in Franklin County in southeastern Idaho and had lived the first winters there in wagon boxes until log homes could be built.

Ezra's father was of the same hardworking stock. He wasted no time teaching his children how to run the eighty-acre farm where Ezra was reared. Each morning George Benson would call to the upstairs bedroom, "Ezra! Time to get chores done," and he'd give the heavy wood stove directly beneath the children's room a hard rattle. That was the sign that Ezra and his brothers and sisters had better get up.

At age four, Ezra, standing up as tall and straight as he could, would take hold of the leather reins and drive a team of horses pulling a plow. He milked several of the family's seventeen Holstein cows twice each day. At age seven, he was digging potatoes, thinning sugar beets, and caring for the Benson's eight work horses. He grew to love the land and the farming life, a trait that would someday help him become the country's most important farm leader.

Ezra was also taught to show respect for others. Shortly after he learned how to talk, Ezra's mother once spent an afternoon teaching him to greet people with a polite "How do you do?" That evening, as the family and a few visiting relatives sat around the dinner table, Ezra looked down from his high chair at a bowlful of boiled eggs and said, "How do you do, eggs?"

As Ezra grew up, he witnessed the arrival of many modern conveniences. He never forgot the tears of joy his mother shed the day she turned a tap in the kitchen and water came out. Until that day the family's water had to be pumped (and pumped and pumped . . .) from a well outside. When he was a teenager, Ezra went with his father to the forest to cut down trees for telephone poles and haul them to the farmhouse. With the help of a technician, he and his father strung the wires and installed their first telephone. Country life seemed much easier with these new inventions.

Ezra's parents knew very well that farm work had to be mixed with fun. After a week of daily farm chores, the family often went to Bear Lake for a day of fishing and swimming, or took a picnic of fried chicken, salads, and homemade ice cream to the canyon. The children also enjoyed footraces, playing with newborn puppies or calves, playing basketball with their father, and sleigh riding in the wintertime. Ezra occasionally tied a long rope around the saddle horn and skied behind his horse. He loved playing marbles and was a local champ. One summer he started out with ten marbles and won well over a thousand.

Even when the Benson children were ill, there were ways of cheering them up. When they all came down with the chicken pox, Ezra's Scottish grandmother, Margaret Dunkley, danced the Highland Fling outside on the lawn to entertain the children. They watched through the front window, squealing with delight.

Halloween brought out the mischief in Ezra. He soon grew to be a tall, husky, robust boy, and he and his pals daringly moved outhouses from where they belonged, scared other Whitney children with sheets over their heads, and once left a farmer's buggy on top of a nearby hill. Ezra seemed to know how to have fun without losing the respect of others. A boyhood friend remembered:

> Ezra T. was always a fellow who liked to have a good time. He always had a lot of fun in everything he did. And at a social he just had a way of mixing in with people, and they'd all have a good time. I think most of the boys in Whitney that were younger looked up to him and felt that he was a real good fellow and would give them good advice.

Fun was fun, but on Sundays, when all work ceased on the Benson farm, a different kind of fun was in order. The family attended Church in the one-room, rock meetinghouse in Whitney. Preparations for the Sabbath began Saturday night when shoes were shined and the children's clothing was laid out. With eleven children to get ready, there was no time to search for socks or shoes Sunday morning. George Benson was determined to be to Church on time and often pulled the buggy out of the yard as a child or two came racing out of the house with shoes or coat in hand.

Ezra's parents were devoted members of the Church and taught their children the principles of the gospel. Ezra came in from the fields one day to find his mother bent over the ironing board with perspiration on her forehead. He asked what she was ironing. "These are my temple clothes, Son." She put her iron down, sat by her son, and took time to explain the importance of the temple and its ordinances. This experience with his mother became a sweet memory for him.

Ezra was baptized and confirmed a member of the Church on August 4, 1907, on his eighth birthday. Five years later his life was again changed when his father was called on a mission to the Northern States. Ezra would now have to take on extra chores and responsibilities to help his mother, who was expecting her eighth child.

While George Benson was on his mission, Ezra helped his brothers and sisters with their schoolwork. He traded milk and eggs at the store in Whitney for other groceries for the family. Meals were kept simple to save money to send to their father. The family often sat down to an evening meal of bread and milk topped with raw onions. This meal became one of Ezra's lifelong favorite snacks, and he often declared, "You know, the onion is the world's most neglected vegetable."

Ezra later said, "Those days on the farm when Father was away [on his mission] were a real test for the family. But there came into our home a spirit of missionary work that never left it." Indeed, the children loved to sit around the kitchen table while their mother read letters she had received from their father. Through his letters, they heard him bear his testimony and tell of his spiritual experiences. In time, all eleven of the Benson children would serve missions; some more than one.

The future prophet attended elementary school in Whitney and later attended high school at the Oneida Stake Academy in Preston, Idaho. Being tall and athletic, Ezra was a valuable member of the school basketball team, which played against other teams from schools in the Snake River Valley. Games were

When George Benson was called on a mission, his wife, Sarah, and his seven children remained behind. Ezra Taft Benson, about age twelve, is standing behind his mother to the left. Photographer unknown.

sometimes played in makeshift locations. In Shelley, Idaho, for example, where there was no basketball court, they drained the swimming pool and attached temporary backboards on either end. One advantage was that the ball couldn't go out of bounds. By participating in sports, "I learned to play fair," Ezra later said. "Father always said 'It's better to lose than lose your temper.' "

Ezra Taft Benson as a young man about the time of his mission. Photographer unknown.

Ezra had several ways of earning extra spending money. He would set muskrat traps on his way to school, checking them on the way home and skinning any muskrats he caught. He dried the pelts and sold them to a fur house in Chicago. He also "hired out" to thin sugar beets for other farmers. He once thinned a whole acre of beets in one day. The farmer was so delighted that he paid Ezra two five-dollar gold pieces and two silver dollars. He went home feeling like the richest man in town.

Ezra continued his education by attending the Utah State Agricultural College in Logan (now Utah State University) for one year. There he first caught sight of Flora Amussen as she zoomed by on Main Street in a Ford convertible. He decided right then and there he wanted to date her, but his cousin said, "Like heck you will. She's too popular for a farm boy."

Flora was indeed a "city girl," the daughter of a Danish-immigrant jeweler and watchmaker. She and her widowed mother lived in a large home where Flora had been brought up to be cultured and refined. On campus she was studentbody vice-president, Girls' Athletic Club president, and a tennis champion. This made Ezra, or "Taft" as he was now called, even more interested. He asked her out for a date, and she accepted. It was the beginning of a courtship that lasted seven years.

During that time, Ezra was ordained an elder and served an honorable mission for the Church in Great Britain from 1921 to 1923. Upon his return, he decided that Flora was the one he wanted to marry. But before he could officially propose to her, Flora made an announcement—she was going on a mission to the Hawaiian Islands! Ezra was shocked. "I was ready to settle down on the farm. It was really tough. She was the light of my life."

Ezra waited. While Flora was away, he busied himself by attending Brigham Young University in Provo, where he was voted Most Popular Man during his senior year. He worked on the farm in Whitney during the summers, where he devised a slogan for the bottles of milk he and his brother sold from their dairy: "You can whip our cream but you can't beat our milk."

With so much to do, the time passed quickly, and soon Flora was home. They were married September 10, 1926, in the Salt Lake Temple. Ezra wrote: "The wedding ceremony was too beautiful for words. Everything went off so quiet and peaceful. It all made us so thankful for the Restored Gospel and all that it holds out to us. Surely we had never been happier."

Together at last, Ezra and Flora began adventures that would take them across the country and all over the world. It would have been impossible for them to know at that time the remarkable experiences awaiting them.

After their marriage, Ezra and Flora traveled in a Model T Ford truck to attend school at Iowa State College, where Ezra graduated with a master's degree. Returning to Whitney, Ezra farmed and worked as an agricultural agent. He taught farmers how to get better crops by using good seed and getting rid of weeds, insects, and annoying rodents. He taught them how to keep careful records of their expenses and to take better care of their machinery and livestock.

In 1929, they moved to Boise, the Idaho state capital, where Ezra was head of the new Department of Agricultural Economics and Marketing. He traveled all over Idaho "helping farmers solve a hundred and one problems." Ezra was soon in demand, giving hundreds of speeches and demonstrations and giving farmers encouragement. He also served as an LDS stake president in Boise, which allowed him to contribute in spiritual ways to the community.

Word was spreading about this energetic young agent who was so skilled in working with people and finding solutions to their farming problems. In 1939, Ezra was appointed executive-secretary of the National Council of Farmers Cooperatives, an organization representing over two million farmers throughout the country. This new job meant moving to the nation's capital, Washington, D.C. While working for the government there, he was again called to serve as a stake president.

Ezra and Flora became the parents of six children, four daughters, and two sons. Their family was very close. "Some of the sweetest experiences of my life are associated with home and family ties," he said many times. Ezra frequently played ball with his two sons, worked with his children in their vegetable garden, and often took one or more of them with him on a business trip. "How fun it was to be with Dad, just him and me," one son said after a trip to Salt Lake City. "We stayed in a hotel and ate in a restaurant together. We talked about anything I wanted to talk about. I knew Dad loved me because he was with me."

Ezra Taft Benson, the man who loved his family, the land, his country, his Church, and the Lord was called to be an apostle in 1943. Church President Heber J. Grant was very old and feeble at this time. He sat in a chair while Ezra knelt down in front of him on the floor to be ordained by the prophet to this new important calling.

In 1946, as an apostle, Ezra became president of the European Mission, headquartered in London. He reopened missions that had been closed during World War II. He organized the shipment of food, clothing, and medicine to the Saints in Europe who were still suffering from the terrible destruction of that war. Many places where Church members had held their meetings had been destroyed or needed major repairs. Ezra found that the

Ezra Taft Benson served as U.S. Secretary of Agriculture from 1952 to 1961. Photograph courtesy of U.S. Department of Agriculture.

Saints needed scriptures and other Church literature, and he arranged for them to be printed or sent. Ezra was often moved to tears when he saw how badly these dear members needed help.

After Ezra returned to the United States, U.S. President Dwight D. Eisenhower appointed him to be Secretary of Agriculture, and Ezra became a member of the president's Cabinet. For eight years he continued on a national scale the work he had begun in Idaho, helping the United States to lead the way as the major producer of food in the world. Ezra was grateful for this opportunity to serve his country. One evening as he strolled along the streets of Washington, D.C., he felt very happy:

> As I walked, I reviewed in my own mind the history of this, the greatest nation under heaven. I presume that never in my life has there come to my heart such a feeling of gratitude and thanksgiving for my citizenship in this land, choice above all others.

It wasn't easy. There was always someone who disagreed with some decision or policy. But Ezra remained strong and true to his convictions, and he was greatly admired for that. One of his assistants once urged him to "remember always that many of your friends feel that a great source of your personal strength is that you walk beside God, whereas most of us only report to him."

The Benson family returned to Salt Lake City in 1961, and Ezra took up again his full-time service as an apostle. Upon the death of Spencer W. Kimball, Ezra Taft Benson was ordained and set apart as the thirteenth president of the Church on November 10, 1985. He was then eighty-six years old. At a press conference, President Benson had a special message for the world: "I love all our Father's children of every color, creed, and

Ezra Taft Benson at the fireside commemorating seventy-five years of Church sponsorship of the Boy Scouts of America. Photographer unknown.

political persuasion. My only desire is to serve as the Lord would have me do." This was, and always had been, President Benson's greatest desire—to serve the Lord and do his will.

The members of the Church welcomed their new prophet with open arms and felt the spirit and power of this great man. One missionary wrote of the time he and his companion met President Benson after a sacrament meeting:

As President Benson approached us, my heart burned.

His glowing, happy face filled our hearts with peace and love. He was so happy to see us! He took our hands in his and held them tight. . . . Never have I felt such penetrating power from a man. Not since my conversion [to the gospel] have I felt so drained by the Spirit. I will never forget it.

"Read the Book of Mormon" became a theme of President Benson's years as a prophet, seer, and revelator. He felt inspired by the Lord to challenge Latter-day Saints of all ages to read the Book of Mormon each day and live by its teachings. "There is a power in the book which will begin to flow into your lives the moment you begin a serious study of the book," he promised.

On May 30, 1994, at the age of ninety-four, President Benson died in his apartment in Salt Lake City. He had served as a General Authority for fifty years, more than half his life. He was buried in Whitney, Idaho.

Throughout his life President Benson traveled many thousands of miles and visited dozens of countries. But the land that once was the Benson family farm in Whitney, Idaho, remained one of his favorite places in all the world, for it was there that he learned as a boy to love his God and his country.

Howard W. Hunter

An Eagle Scout Who Learned by Doing

Eleven-year-old Howard W. Hunter had just enjoyed one of the best Christmases ever. The year was 1918, and the gifts "Santa Claus" had left for him included a sled, a Scout knife, a tie, and a heavy woolen coat. The Christmas dinner that followed seemed like a feast, and Howard summed up the day by proclaiming in his journal, "We had everything good there was."

Howard's childhood in Boise, Idaho, seemed to fit the same description as that Christmas Day many years ago. He seemed to be surrounded by everything good there was: a close-knit family, jobs that built his self-confidence, and a variety of dearly loved pets.

Howard William Hunter was born on November 14, 1907, in Boise, Idaho. He was the first of two children born to John William (Will) Hunter and Nellie Marie Rasmussen Hunter. Howard's sister, Dorothy, was born two years later in 1909. She and Howard would remain the best of friends throughout their lives.

Howard's parents were descendants of converts to The

Church of Jesus Christ of Latter-day Saints from Scotland, Scandinavia, and the United States. Will and Nellie met in Boise, where Nellie was living with relatives. They were married in Nellie's hometown of Mount Pleasant, Utah, on December 3, 1906. They returned to live in Boise, where Will worked for an interurban railroad company that delivered mail and passengers to several communities west of the city. Nellie was a hardworking homemaker who added to the family income by working part-time at a dry-cleaning company and demonstrating White King soap. She tried always to be at home when the children were out of school. Nellie volunteered much of her time to Scouting, selling war bonds, and fulfilling her church callings.

As a young boy, Howard loved nature and the outdoors. Within half a mile of where the Hunters lived, the Boise River ran through the city. There was a wooded area there that Howard loved to visit after school and on Saturdays. Together with his dog, a fox terrier named Daisy, he sailed boats, saw beavers build dams, made whistles out of willows, and watched fish swim in the river. He especially enjoyed watching birds build nests and hatch their young.

If there was ever a boy who wished he had grown up on a farm, it was Howard. He secretly envied children who lived in the country, feeling sure that they had more fun and more interesting chores than boys and girls who had been raised in the city.

When he was out of school during the summer, Howard loved visiting his aunt and uncle who owned a ranch at Barber, a sawmill town northeast of Boise. There his cousins taught him to ride horses and to swim. They picked berries and gathered eggs from the chicken coops, then drove a horse-drawn buggy into Barber to sell their products door-to-door.

Howard W. Hunter at about one year and five years of age.

During one of his visits to the ranch, however, five-year-old Howard began to miss his parents as the days went by. He became homesick and later wrote, "I went down the orchard into the grape vineyard where no one could see me cry."

Part of the attraction of being outside for Howard was his love of animals. He had a special place in his heart for animals that had been abandoned or mistreated. "Every stray cat could find a haven at our house," he said, "even against family objections." One day some neighborhood boys found a stray kitten and entertained themselves by putting it into a sack and throwing it into the canal. When the kitten crawled out, they threw it in again. The boys soon grew tired of their mischief, and Howard stepped in and rescued the cat. He took it home, where his mother lined a box with a quilt and put the box under the stove, where it was warm. The cat soon dried out, recovered from its ordeal, and lived with the Hunter family for many years.

Howard had a pet dog, and he enjoyed keeping rabbits, which he would occasionally let run loose on the lawn to nibble on the grass. His two favorite rabbits were Bunny Boo and Mary Jane.

By the time Howard was a teenager, he had earned money at an amazing variety of jobs. Clearly it was important to Will and Nellie Hunter that their son learn to work. When Howard was only two years old, his father put a small hammer in his hand and had him pound nails into the floorboards of a new home they were building in Boise. Later, Howard was found cutting lawns, polishing the kitchen stove, feeding chickens and cleaning their coops, picking fruit, and selling newspapers on the street after school. Howard quickly lost a job weeding the family potato patch when he hoed down all the potatoes his father had recently planted.

Other jobs Howard had while growing up included delivering telegrams, preparing ice cream sundaes at a pharmacy soda fountain, delivering prescriptions by bicycle, writing ads and preparing billings for a newspaper, framing pictures in an art store, selling shoes, and performing a variety of tasks at Boise's finest hotel, the Idanha. Howard had little time for mischief—he was too busy.

An important part of Howard's social life was his participation in church activities with his friends in their small Boise ward. Howard's mother was the Primary president, and she later became president of the young women's organization. She played an important role in teaching the gospel to Howard and his sister, Dorothy. Howard's father, a fine man, was not a member of the Church and felt that his two children should be older before they made a decision whether or not to be baptized. Hence, Howard and Dorothy were not baptized when they became eight years old. Howard wrote:

> I did have a testimony, though. I knew that God lived. My mother had taught me to pray and to thank Heavenly Father for all the things that I enjoyed. I often thanked Him for the beauty of the earth and for the wonderful times that I had at the ranch and by the river and with the Scouts. I also learned to ask Him for the things that I wanted or needed. It wasn't until I was twelve that I really missed . . . being baptized. By that time, all my friends had been ordained deacons. Because I wasn't an official member of the Church, I wasn't able to do many of the things that they did. Passing the sacrament and building a fire to warm up the meeting house were only two of the responsibilities that I watched my friends do without me.
>
> So my sister and I began coaxing our father to allow us to be baptized. We also prayed that he might say yes. We were overjoyed when he finally gave his consent, and I was baptized.

Howard and Dorothy were baptized on April 4, 1920, in the Natatorium, a large indoor swimming complex in Boise. He was twelve years old, and his sister was ten.

Seven years later, on February 6, 1927, Howard's father was baptized a member of The Church of Jesus Christ of Latter-day Saints. Howard, Dorothy, and of course their mother were thrilled.

Three years after Howard's baptism, an event occurred

that caused the people of his ward to admire him. The ward badly needed a new meetinghouse to replace the aging frame building in which they were meeting. A tabernacle would be built to serve both the stake and the ward. When ward members were asked to pledge what they could afford to support the project, a fifteen-year-old boy rose to his feet and said, "I'm Howard Hunter, and I pledge twenty-five dollars." He had worked hard to save that money, but he knew the new building was worth the sacrifice. Others followed his example. The money was found, and the tabernacle was built.

Howard became active in the Boy Scouts of America. He attended a variety of Scout camps, working hard on merit badge requirements. On May 12, 1923, when Howard was fifteen years old, the following article appeared in the *Idaho Statesman:*

> Howard Hunter of troop 22, Boise council, Boy Scouts of America, having qualified for merit badges in 32 subjects, was honored Friday at the city hall by the court of honor of the Boise council, with the degree of "eagle scout." . . . The honor attained by Scout Hunter is the highest in scouting, and he is the second Boise scout to reach this rank.

As Howard entered his teenage years, music became an important part of his life. Blessed with rare perfect pitch, Howard learned to play the piano, violin, saxophone, clarinet, trumpet, and drums, and a marimba he had won in a contest. Before Howard was out of high school, he formed a dance band called "Hunter's Croonaders," which played at many gatherings throughout the Boise area.

Upon his graduation from high school in 1927, his five-

Howard (center, holding saxophone) and his band in 1927.

member band was hired to play on a cruise ship, the SS *President Jackson.* They spent ten weeks performing aboard the ship and visiting ports in Japan, China, and the Philippines. This was a thrilling adventure for a young man who had seen little of the world outside of Idaho and Utah. One day while touring the Orient, Howard purchased a monkey, thinking it would be a fun pet. Yet the monkey had to stay in Howard's small cabin on the ship, and that caused a few problems. Howard quickly noticed the monkey was noisy and smelly. One day Howard returned to his cabin to find that the monkey had opened his suitcase and thrown his clothes all over the room! Howard had to get rid of the monkey.

Upon returning home from his cruise to the Orient, Howard decided to move to southern California, where he worked at a bank, took some college classes, and played with a local dance band. His parents and sister eventually joined him in Los Angeles.

In March 1930, Howard asked his stake patriarch, George T. Wride, for a patriarchal blessing. In that blessing young Howard was informed that he was one "whom the Lord foreknew" and that he had been ordained "to perform an important work in mortality." During these years, Howard began to study the gospel more seriously. A special Sunday School teacher had a great influence on him:

> Although I had attended Church classes most of my life, my first real awakening to the gospel came in a Sunday School class in Adams Ward taught by Brother Peter A. Clayton. He had a wealth of knowledge and the ability to inspire young people. I studied the lessons, read the outside assignments he gave us, and participated in speaking on assigned subjects. I suddenly became aware of the real meaning of some of the gospel principles, an understanding of the degrees of glory, and the requirements of celestial exaltation as Brother Clayton taught and instructed us. I think of this period of my life as the time the truths of the gospel commenced to unfold. I always had a testimony of the gospel, but suddenly I commenced to understand.

At a church dance, Howard met Clara (Claire) May Jeffs. She was a fashion model and an assistant manager at a large department store in Los Angeles. Howard was immediately

Howard and Claire in their courting days.

interested in her and said to Claire, "Why don't you ever go
out with me?" She said, "Why don't you ask me?" Soon they
were dating. Three years later they were married on June 10,
1931, in the Salt Lake Temple.

Howard had other important decisions to make. Although
he had enjoyed his work as a musician, he decided that the
late-night jobs and after-hours atmosphere would not permit

the kind of family life he wanted. He packed his instruments away and took them out again only for private family gatherings.

When Howard and Claire were married, they made a commitment to stay out of debt and buy things only after they had saved the money they needed. For instance, Claire scrubbed their clothes on a washboard until they could afford a washing machine.

After a few years of working at a bank and at various other jobs, Howard decided he wanted to be a lawyer, and after five years of schooling, he graduated from the Southwestern University Law School in Los Angeles in 1939. He enjoyed helping people and businesses and became one of the most respected and admired attorneys in southern California. Howard often offered free legal advice to those who couldn't afford to pay him for his services. His law clients trusted his honest and wise advice. His honorable reputation led to Howard being asked to serve on the boards of directors of more than two dozen companies.

Howard and Claire became the parents of three sons: Howard William, Jr. (who died as a baby), John Jacob, and Richard Allen. Howard was a good father. Together the family enjoyed building model trains, going to the beach, and making homemade kayaks.

Howard devoted many hours to helping his sons earn their camping merit badges, which required them to sleep out in the open for fifty nights. John Hunter remembers an adventurous night when he and Richard and their father stopped their car and rolled their sleeping bags out in a convenient spot. They awakened in the middle of the night to see a herd of moose sniffing around their campsite. Another night, the three of them woke up suddenly at the sound and light of a train coming straight at them! A few yards away, the train changed direction, passing within twenty feet of the terrified campers. In the dark, they had set up their camp too close to a railroad track.

Howard served the Church faithfully and energetically all his life. At age 32, he was called to serve as bishop of the El Sereno Ward, and after that he served as president of the Pasadena Stake.

One of the most wonderful days in Howard Hunter's life was his forty-sixth birthday. On that day he and Claire participated in a Pasadena Stake excursion to the Arizona Temple in Mesa. As they assembled in the chapel, the temple president called on Howard to speak. After a few minutes, Howard looked up from the podium to see his parents walk into the chapel, dressed in white. They had never been to a temple before. On that day Will and Nellie were endowed, and then Howard knelt with his parents around a sacred altar and they were sealed together as an eternal family. Nearly three years later, Howard's sister, Dorothy, was sealed to them in the just-completed Los Angeles Temple.

Howard W. Hunter was called to be a member of the Quorum of the Twelve Apostles in 1959. This important call required a great deal of sacrifice. He gave up his hard-earned law practice and left friends in California that he and Claire had known for many years. They accepted the call without hesitation, but with a great deal of humility. He served as an apostle for nearly thirty-six years.

Reflecting on his years as a General Authority, Elder Hunter said: "One of my prized assignments was adviser to the Primary, where I served for about ten years. I visited Primaries all over the world and never missed an opportunity to visit a Primary group."

Claire, Howard, Louine, and John, with the Hunters' first grand-child, Robert Mark.

While traveling throughout the world as an apostle of the Lord, Elder Hunter endured a tropical storm as he traveled by boat in Tonga, escaped a mugging attempt in Panama, pushed a car through a blizzard in Norway, and shared living quarters in Poland with flies, dogs, cats, chickens, and geese. He encountered deadly snakes and rough trails in Mexico and

Howard W. Hunter carves turkey for Christmas dinner at John's home in 1983.

Guatemala. Still, he greatly enjoyed the adventure and education these trips brought to his life.

Elder Hunter's wife, Claire, was ill for several years before she died on October 9, 1983. Six and a half years later, on April 10, 1990, he married Inis Egan, a widow and long-time friend from California.

As Howard Hunter passed eighty years of age, his

physical strength declined, even as his spiritual and mental strength grew. At the April 1988 general conference, he lost his balance while speaking at the podium in the Tabernacle. He fell backwards into a flower arrangement, but he was immediately helped up by his fellow apostles and continued his talk. A medical examination later showed that he had broken three ribs in the fall.

At noon, members of the Hunter family gathered in his office for lunch together. The Hunter grandchildren, who had a close and loving relationship with their grandfather, teased him about what had happened. "Yeah, Grandpa, you just wanted more attention," one said. Another joked by saying, "Your talk wasn't good enough so you had to do something to make it better." Grandfather Hunter leaned back on his office chair and roared with laughter.

President Hunter not only knew how to endure pain without complaining, he was also brave in the face of danger. In February 1993, he was about to address a nineteen-stake fireside at Brigham Young University when a man carrying a briefcase rushed onto the stage and ordered everyone off but President Hunter, whom he commanded to read a written statement. President Hunter calmly but firmly refused. The man indicated that he had a bomb in his briefcase.

A few students, and then the entire audience, began to sing "We Thank Thee, O God, for a Prophet." The intruder was distracted, giving security officers a chance to restrain the man. When things calmed down, President Hunter rested a few moments only before giving his talk as if nothing had happened. He read from his prepared talk, "Life has a fair number of challenges," and added, "as demonstrated." The briefcase was later opened by police; there was no bomb inside.

Howard William Hunter was ordained and set apart as the fourteenth president of The Church of Jesus Christ of Latter-day Saints on June 5, 1994. Although he would serve as the prophet for only nine months, President Hunter's influence would be felt throughout the world. His sweet, humble spirit would touch the lives of the members of the Church from the first moments of his presidency when he spoke these words:

> I have shed many tears and have sought my Father in Heaven in earnest prayer with a desire to be equal to the high and holy calling which is now mine.
>
> My greatest strength through these past hours and recent days has been my abiding testimony that this is the work of God and not men, that Jesus Christ is the authorized and living head of this church and He leads it in word and deed. I pledge my life, my strength, and the full measure of my soul to serving Him fully. . . .
>
> I would invite all members of the Church to live with ever more attention to the life and example of the Lord Jesus Christ, especially the love and hope and compassion he displayed.
>
> I pray that we might treat each other with more kindness, more courtesy, more humility and patience and forgiveness. . . .
>
> I also invite the members of the Church to establish the temple of the Lord as the great symbol of their membership and the supernal setting for their most sacred covenants. It would be the deepest desire of my heart to have every member of the Church be temple worthy.

Even though he suffered from many health problems relating to a heart attack, back surgery, and cancer, President Hunter used every minute of his presidency to visit and inspire the Latter-day Saints. During these few short months, he traveled to Illinois, Arizona, California, Switzerland, and Mexico.

His last public appearance was in January 1995, when he dedicated the Bountiful Utah Temple. He was hospitalized shortly afterwards and was told that his cancer had worsened. He had endured to the end. President Howard William Hunter died on March 3, 1995, at his home in Salt Lake City.

At his funeral, which was held in the Salt Lake Tabernacle, his former stake president Jon Huntsman spoke as if he were talking directly to President Hunter when he said:

> Thank you, dear President, for loving the Savior so deeply. You spent your life learning of him and speaking of him. *He was your best friend.* You helped us become closer to our elder Brother. . . . You became so much like him. You gave hope to all of us who stumble as you gently lifted us and offered the light and the way. You provided a vital glimpse of your "sure knowledge" when near the end you sweetly stated, "Let's look for each other on the other side." . . . You are our hero. We love you forever and ever.

The new president of the Quorum of the Twelve in 1988.

Gordon B. Hinckley

"Forget Yourself and Go to Work"

Early in his life, Bryant Stringham Hinckley had good reason to believe his life was being protected. He had two frightening experiences during his youth that could easily have taken his life.

On one occasion, young Bryant was accidentally shot in the leg by his brother Ed, who was examining a pistol that he thought was not loaded. As blood streamed down Bryant's leg, his father sent one of the boys for a doctor. The bullet had lodged somewhere above his left knee but was never found. Many nights thereafter, when the pain was intense, Bryant's father would take him in his arms and walk the floor and comfort him.

On another occasion, Bryant took a trip with his father from Fillmore, Utah, to nearby Cove Fort. The two were riding in a fine carriage pulled by two stallions named Warfield and Prince. They stopped to rest along the way, and Bryant's father removed the bit from the mouth of one horse to see if it would drink from a bucket of water. Suddenly, the horses bolted and raced down the bumpy, dusty road, with Bryant in the buggy hanging on for dear life. He leaped out just seconds before the horses jumped a fence and smashed the buggy. Bryant hit the ground with a terrific blow, but again his life was spared.

Why this protection? There may have been many reasons for the Lord to watch over him. But consider this: Bryant Stringham Hinckley, born in Coalville, Utah, in 1867, was to become the father of a latter-day prophet.

Bryant continued to face and overcome difficulties as the Lord prepared him to become a prophet's father. Years later, at the age of forty-one, he faced a challenge even bigger than bullet wounds and runaway horses. His first wife, Christine Johnson, died of appendicitis, leaving Bryant alone with eight children to care for.

After Christine's death, Bryant met Ada Bitner. Both Bryant and Ada were teaching at the Salt Lake Business College (later known as the LDS Business College). Ada taught English and shorthand classes and was a talented musician. Their friendship deepened, and they were married in the Salt Lake Temple on August 4, 1909. The oldest of their five children, Gordon Bitner Hinckley, became the fifteenth president of The Church of Jesus Christ of Latter-day Saints.

Gordon was born June 23, 1910, in Salt Lake City. He would later describe himself as "a pale-faced, spindly sort of a child." Pale-faced and spindly he may have been, but he received deeply felt spiritual experiences early. Just after Gordon was ordained a deacon, he and his father attended their first stake priesthood meeting together one evening in the Salt Lake Tenth Ward chapel. Bryant was first counselor in the Salt Lake Liberty Stake presidency and made his way to the front to sit on the stand. Gordon sat on the back row. The chapel was filled with priesthood brethren, many of whom were converts from Europe and

Gordon B. Hinckley as an Aaronic Priesthood holder.

had sacrificed much for their membership in the Church. As the meeting began, every man in attendance stood and sang the opening song:

> Praise to the man who communed with Jehovah!
> Jesus anointed that Prophet and Seer.
> Blessed to open the last dispensation,
> Kings shall extol him, and nations revere.
> (*Hymns*, 1985, no. 27)

Gordon later recalled: "It touched my heart. It gave me a feeling that was difficult to describe. I'd never had it previously in terms of any Church experience. There came into my heart a conviction that the man of whom they sang was really a prophet of God. I'm grateful to be able to say that that conviction, which came I believe by the power of the Holy Spirit, has never left me."

The Hinckley family lived for a time in the Salt Lake First Ward. Their two-story house sat on a large corner lot. It seemed to Gordon that the many trees in their yard shed millions of leaves, which required an immense amount of work each fall. Their modest but comfortable home included a special room they called the library. The room contained an oak study table, a good lamp, and more than a thousand books: literature, science, histories, maps, and encyclopedias. Although Gordon didn't spend all his time reading, his parents did introduce him to the value of good books. As an adult he would have a great love of reading and learning, for which he always thanked his parents.

As a child, Gordon survived a serious case of whooping cough. The family doctor suggested he needed fresh country air to fully recover his health. Bryant and Ada decided to buy several acres of farmland in East Mill Creek in the Salt Lake Valley. They lived in town while school was in session and then spent their summers in the country, planting trees, irrigating, and raising a garden. Gordon recovered from his illness and enjoyed the wide open spaces. He later wrote:

> I learned to live around animals and learned the lessons of nature—the beauty that is there and the penalties that come when nature is abused.
>
> We had large fruit orchards, and we learned how to prune trees. . . .

In January, February, and March we pruned the trees, but we didn't like it, because it was hard work. Yet we did learn something from it: You can determine the kind of fruit crop that you will have in September by the way you prune the trees in February. That was a great lesson, and it applies to people as well. You can pretty much determine the kind of adults you will have by the way you care for them as children.

With no television or radio, the Hinckley children found endless other ways to have fun. They enjoyed sledding and skating on the pond at a neighborhood park. They loved sleeping out at night and finding the North Star among the millions of twinkling lights. During his boyhood, Gordon's self-confidence grew as he learned practical skills that would benefit him the rest of his life. He learned how to use tools to do plumbing, carpentry, and electrical work. Years later, Gordon was able to build a comfortable and cozy new home for his own family.

As a six-year-old boy, Gordon seemed more excited about hands-on work than leaving his siblings and going to school. Shy and greatly attached to his younger siblings, he was hesitant to begin this new phase of life. He convinced his parents to let him stay home another year. When he was seven, his parents were more insistent, but Gordon refused to go to school and hid from his parents on the first day of class. They finally found him and took him crying to school. As it turned out, Gordon quickly learned to enjoy school, and he skipped two grades to be able to attend with those of his own age-group.

While in the seventh grade, Gordon and his friends decided to skip school for a day. The boys were protesting a decision by the administration to leave the seventh graders at the elementary school that year rather than advance them to the junior high school, which was already too crowded. To show their frustration, they spent the school day wandering around town. When Gordon returned the next day for class, the principal wouldn't allow him back in the building without a note from his parents. Gordon returned home, told his mother what he had done, and stood quietly while she wrote a short note:

Dear Mr. Stearns,

    Please excuse Gordon's absence yesterday. His action was simply an impulse to follow the crowd.

Gordon's mother signed the note and handed it to him. It taught him an important lesson. Gordon remembered how he felt when he returned to meet the principal:

    I walked back over to school and got there about the same time a few other boys did. We all handed our notes to Mr. Stearns. I do not know whether he read them, but I have never forgotten my mother's note. Though I had been an active party to the action we had taken, I resolved then and there that I would never do anything on the basis of simply following the crowd. I determined then and there that I would make my own decisions on the basis of their merits and my standards and not be pushed in one direction or another by those around me.

Gordon was a successful and eager student. He attended the Hamilton School for the first seven grades, then Roosevelt Junior High School and LDS High School. He graduated from the University of Utah in 1932 with a major in English and a minor in ancient languages. Gordon was grateful for his education. Many years later, in 1971, he was

honored to receive the University of Utah Distinguished
Alumnus Award.

Great sorrow came into Gordon's life when he was twenty
years old. His mother was diagnosed with cancer and died at
the age of fifty. Gordon's father had taken her to Los Angeles
during her illness for better medical treatment and she died
there while hospitalized. Gordon tells of his father's return to
Salt Lake City:

> I remember with clarity my brokenhearted father as he
> stepped off the train and greeted his grief-stricken chil-
> dren. We walked solemnly down the station platform to
> the baggage car, where the casket was unloaded and
> taken by the mortician. We came to know even more
> about the tenderness of our father's heart. This has had
> an effect on me all of my life.
>
> I also came to know something of death—the absolute
> devastation of children losing their mother—but also of
> peace without pain, and the certainty that death cannot
> be the end of the soul.

Gordon's plans to attend Columbia University in New
York to study journalism were changed in 1933 when he
received a call to serve in the European Mission, with head-
quarters in London, England. At this time, the United States
was in the middle of the great financial depression. Like
many Americans, Gordon lost virtually all his hard-earned
money when the bank in which he had deposited his savings
failed. A mission now seemed impossible, but the Lord provided a way for him to go. In addition to money Gordon's
father and brother contributed, his mission was financed by
a savings account his now-deceased mother had wisely and

Gordon B. Hinckley as a missionary in London, England.

secretly kept. Gordon always considered the money his
mother had saved as very sacred.

The first months of Gordon's mission to England were
filled with loneliness and discouragement. At one point he

wrote home to his father saying he wanted to come home. Bryant wrote back to his missionary son with this simple suggestion: "Forget yourself and go to work." This advice changed Gordon's attitude and proved to be a turning point in his life. He soon found himself confidently facing all kinds of missionary situations with courage and faith: conducting street meetings, answering difficult gospel questions, and ironing out problems with the local press.

During his two years in England, Gordon served in Preston, Lancashire. He was then called to serve in the European Mission office in London as assistant to the mission president, Joseph F. Merrill.

Completing his mission and returning home, Gordon began a lifetime of service to The Church of Jesus Christ of Latter-day Saints. At the request of the First Presidency, he went to work as secretary of the Radio, Publicity, and Literature Committee of the Church. He wrote hundreds of scripts for radio, filmstrips, and movies. He prepared pamphlets and mission materials. For a young man who loved words, Gordon had found work that suited him perfectly. Later, at the age of twenty-seven, Gordon was called to serve as a member of the Sunday School General Board. As part of this assignment, he wrote a manual for the study of the Book of Mormon. It was used in Sunday Schools throughout the Church for more than two decades.

Although he was spending long hours at work, Gordon began to pay closer attention to Marjorie Pay, a young lady he had grown up with. He had first met her while the two of them attended Primary as children. Gordon and Marjorie renewed their friendship at a Church dance, courted, and were married in the Salt Lake Temple on April 29, 1937.

Marjorie was impressed with Gordon from the very

Left to right: Virginia Hinckley, Clark Hinckley, Marjorie Hinckley, Gordon B. Hinckley, Jane Hinckley (girl in front), Heather Barnes (baby), Kathleen Hinckley Barnes, Alan Barnes. 1961.

beginning. "Everything he did, he did with a little flair that was typical of him and no one else," she said. "He had wonderful integrity. You never had to worry about anything he did, or anything he said." They became the parents of five children: Kathleen, Richard, Virginia, Clark, and Jane.

As a father, Gordon hoped to instill a love for Church history in his five children. Both he and Marjorie were descendants of faithful Latter-day Saint pioneers and frequently took their children on family vacations to historical sites in Utah and surrounding areas. "We didn't have a lot of money," said Marjorie, "so we did things that were fun, but not expensive. We saw the state of Utah, every square foot of it."

Virginia remembers that on these trips they "stopped at every historical marker that was ever placed at the side of a highway." Her father knew the history of the Church well, and his storytelling made it come alive for his children. Marjorie read aloud to the children on the long stretches of highway, passing a love of books and literature on to yet another generation of Hinckleys.

Gordon was a great handyman. He built a home for his family in East Mill Creek. He could install a furnace, shingle the roof, or get the family car up and running again. Once, while visiting a friend's house, Gordon's daughter Kathleen was surprised to hear that they had taken a broken kitchen toaster to a repairman. "I was shocked!" remembers Kathleen. "I didn't know there were people who repaired toasters. I thought everyone's father took care of things like that."

During World War II, Gordon wanted to find a way to help with the war effort. He accepted a job as assistant superintendent of the Salt Lake City Union Depot and Railroad Company. The family soon moved to Denver, where Gordon was assigned to work in the head office of the Denver & Rio Grande Western Railroad Company.

When the war was over, however, the LDS Church wanted Gordon back in Salt Lake City. He worked as the executive secretary to the Missionary Department, and his phone rang day and night with calls from mission presidents all over the

Gordon B. Hinckley among youth in South America.

world. One morning when he walked into his office, the phone was already ringing. Before Gordon could take off his hat and coat, he had spoken with mission presidents in South Africa, Europe, and Asia, answering questions, giving advice, and helping solve problems.

In 1954, President David O. McKay asked him to find a way to present the temple ceremony in several languages. This was a huge project, and it led to the presentation of the ceremony in fourteen languages at that time.

In 1956, Gordon was called to serve as president of the East Millcreek Stake. Those who worked with him said they actually looked forward to the many administrative meetings they attended. They knew President Hinckley made good use of the time and got things done. He was also known for a wonderful sense of humor. His telling of humorous stories made their meetings and Church assignments even more enjoyable.

Gordon was called by President McKay to serve as an Assistant to the Council of the Twelve in 1958. Two and a half years later, on September 30, 1961, he was sustained as a member of the Quorum of the Twelve Apostles.

Elder Hinckley's service as an apostle would take him tens of thousands of miles in the service of the Lord and would cover an amazing variety of assignments. He greeted Latter-day Saints and Church leaders in Europe, South America, Asia, the United States, Canada, and Mexico. He helped organize plans and obtain land for temples and schools and hundreds of church meetinghouses. He divided missions and stakes, trained mission presidents, and dedicated countries to the preaching of the gospel. During a short three-year period, from 1983 to 1986, he dedicated eighteen temples. Everywhere he went, Elder Hinckley strengthened and uplifted the Latter-day Saints.

From 1983 to 1995, President Hinckley served as a counselor in the First Presidency to three Church presidents: Spencer W. Kimball, Ezra Taft Benson, and Howard W. Hunter. As each of these presidents experienced age-related illness, President Hinckley shouldered much of the heavy responsibility for the day-to-day administration of the Church.

One of the most emotional assignments for President

Gordon B. Hinckley with three of his grandchildren.

The Hinckleys on Christmas Eve, 1991.

Hinckley came June 12, 1994, when he presided over the ground-breaking ceremonies for a new temple in Preston, Lancashire, England. There, in front of more than ten thousand English members of the Church, he reflected back more than sixty years on his service as a young missionary in that very city: "Never back in those years would I have dreamed that here in Lancashire there would someday stand a House of the Lord and that I would have a part in breaking ground for its construction."

Gordon Bitner Hinckley was ordained and set apart as the fifteenth prophet and president of The Church of Jesus Christ of Latter-day Saints on March 12, 1995. He chose as counselors Thomas S. Monson and James E. Faust.

At the time of President Hinckley's ordination, Elder David B. Haight of the Quorum of the Twelve Apostles said: "President Hinckley has been prepared in a marvelous way. He has been schooled and carefully honed for this wonderful, marvelous call to be God's prophet on the earth." His second counselor, President Faust, said: "I don't know of any single man who has come to the presidency of this Church who has been so well prepared. He has been taught by all of the great leaders of our time, one-on-one."

It seemed easy and natural for the Latter-day Saints to sustain the new prophet on April 1, 1995, at the solemn assembly held in Salt Lake City. Through his decades of service as a General Authority and as a member of the First Presidency, Gordon B. Hinckley's face had become familiar and comforting to millions of members of the Church throughout the world. Not only had he greeted them and counseled with them from the pulpit in the Salt Lake Tabernacle, but he had met with many thousands of them in their own homes and villages.

At the April 1995 general conference of the Church, President Hinckley, who was then eighty-four, offered this challenge to the Latter-day Saints: "We have a work to do, you and I, so very much of it. Let us roll up our sleeves and get at it, with a new commitment, putting our trust in the Lord. . . . We can do it, if we will be prayerful and faithful."

Facts on the Presidents of the Church

PROPHET	BIRTH DATE	BIRTHPLACE
Joseph Smith, Jr.	December 23, 1805	Sharon, Vermont
Brigham Young	June 1, 1801	Whitingham, Vermont
John Taylor	November 1, 1808	Milnthorpe, England
Wilford Woodruff	March 1, 1807	near Hartford, Connecticut
Lorenzo Snow	April 3, 1814	Mantua, Ohio
Joseph F. Smith	November 13, 1838	Far West, Missouri
Heber J. Grant	November 22, 1856	Salt Lake City, Utah
George Albert Smith	April 4, 1870	Salt Lake City, Utah
David O. McKay	September 8, 1873	Huntsville, Utah
Joseph Fielding Smith	July 19, 1876	Salt Lake City, Utah
Harold B. Lee	March 28, 1899	Clifton, Idaho
Spencer W. Kimball	March 28, 1895	Salt Lake City, Utah
Ezra Taft Benson	August 4, 1899	Whitney, Idaho
Howard W. Hunter	November 14, 1907	Boise, Idaho
Gordon B. Hinckley	June 23, 1910	Salt Lake City, Utah

AGE HE BECAME PROPHET		YEARS SERVED	DEATH DATE	PLACE HE DIED
J. Smith, Jr.	24	14	June 27, 1844	Carthage, Illinois
Young	46	30	Aug. 29, 1877	Salt Lake City, Utah
Taylor	71	7	July 25, 1887	Kaysville, Utah
Woodruff	82	9	Sept. 2, 1898	San Francisco, California
Snow	84	3	Oct. 10, 1901	Salt Lake City, Utah
J. F. Smith	62	18	Nov. 19, 1918	Salt Lake City, Utah
Grant	62	26	May 14, 1945	Salt Lake City, Utah
G. A. Smith	75	6	April 4, 1951	Salt Lake City, Utah
McKay	77	19	Jan. 18, 1970	Salt Lake City, Utah
J. Fielding Smith	93	2	July 2, 1972	Salt Lake City, Utah
Lee	73	1	Dec. 26, 1973	Salt Lake City, Utah
Kimball	78	12	Nov. 5, 1985	Salt Lake City, Utah
Benson	86	8	May 30, 1994	Salt Lake City, Utah
Hunter	86	1	March 3, 1995	Salt Lake City, Utah
Hinckley	84	—	—	—

	1800	1820	1840	1860	1880	1900	1920	1940	1960	1980	2000

Joseph Smith, Jr. — (1805) (1830–1844)

Brigham Young — (1801) (1835) (1847–1877)

John Taylor — (1808) (1838) (1880–1887)

Wilford Woodruff — (1807) (1839) (1889–1898)

Lorenzo Snow — (1814) (1849) (1898–1901)

Joseph F. Smith — (1838) (1866) (1901–1918)

Heber J. Grant — (1856) (1882) (1918–1945)

George Albert Smith — (1870) (1903) (1945–1951)

David O. McKay — (1873) (1906) (1951–1970)

Joseph Fielding Smith — (1876) (1910) (1970–1972)

Harold B. Lee — (1899) (1941) (1972–1973)

Spencer W. Kimball — (1895) (1943) (1973–1985)

Ezra Taft Benson — (1899) (1943) (1985–1994)

Howard W. Hunter — (1907) (1959) (1994–1995)

Gordon B. Hinckley — (1910) (1961) (1995–)

Legend: ● Birth — □ Years as Apostle — ■ Years as President of the Church

Bibliography

General Sources

Alexander, Thomas G., and James B. Allen. *Mormons and Gentiles.* Boulder, Colorado: Pruett, 1984.

Allen, James B., and Glen M. Leonard. *The Story of the Latter-day Saints.* Salt Lake City: Deseret Book, 1976.

Arrington, Leonard J., ed. *The Presidents of the Church.* Salt Lake City: Deseret Book, 1986.

Arrington, Leonard J., and Davis Bitton. *The Mormon Experience.* New York: Alfred Knopf, 1979.

Arrington, Leonard J., and Susan Arrington Madsen. *Mothers of the Prophets.* Salt Lake City: Deseret Book, 1987.

At Home with the Prophets (pamphlet). Salt Lake City: The Church of Jesus Christ of Latter-day Saints, 1979.

West, Emerson Roy. *Profiles of the Presidents.* Salt Lake City: Deseret Book, 1972.

Joseph Smith, Jr.

Arrington, Leonard J. "The Human Qualities of Joseph Smith, the Prophet." *Ensign,* January 1971, pp. 35–38.

Bushman, Richard L. *Joseph Smith and the Beginnings of Mormonism.* Urbana and Chicago: University of Illinois Press, 1984.

Hill, Donna. *Joseph Smith, the First Mormon.* New York: Doubleday, 1977.

Porter, Larry C., and Susan Easton Black. *The Prophet Joseph: Essays on the Life and Mission of Joseph Smith.* Salt Lake City: Deseret Book, 1988.

Smith, Lucy Mack. *Biographical Sketches of Joseph Smith the Prophet and His Progenitors for Many Generations.* Liverpool, England: n.p., 1853.

Brigham Young

Arrington, Leonard J. *Brigham Young: American Moses.* New York: Alfred Knopf, 1985.

Irving, Gordon. "Encouraging the Saints: Brigham Young's Annual Tours of Mormon Settlements." *Utah Historical Quarterly* 45 (Summer 1977): 233–51.

Savage, C. R. "A Trip South with President Brigham Young in 1870."

Improvement Era, February 1900, pp. 293–99; March 1900, pp. 363–69; April 1900, pp. 431–36.

Walker, Ronald W., and Ronald K. Esplin. "Brigham Himself: An Autobiographical Recollection." *Journal of Mormon History* 4 (1977): 19–34.

John Taylor

Roberts, B. H. *The Life of John Taylor.* Salt Lake City: Bookcraft, 1963.

Taylor, Samuel W., and Raymond W. Taylor. *The John Taylor Papers: Records of the Last Utah Pioneer.* 2 vols. Redwood City, California: Taylor Trust, Publisher, 1984–85.

Taylor, Samuel W. *The Kingdom or Nothing: The Life of John Taylor, Militant Mormon.* New York: Macmillan Publishing Co., 1976.

Wilford Woodruff

Arrington, James W. *Wilford Woodruff: God's Fisherman.* Play, unpublished.

Gibbons, Francis. *Wilford Woodruff: Wondrous Worker, Prophet of God.* Salt Lake City: Deseret Book, 1988.

Kenney, Scott G., ed. *Wilford Woodruff's Journal, 1833–98.* Typescript. 9 vols. Midvale, Utah: Signature, 1983.

Woodruff, Wilford. *Leaves from My Journal: Third Book of the Faith-Promoting Series.* Salt Lake City: Juvenile Instructor Office, 1881.

Lorenzo Snow

Arrington, Leonard J., Feramorz Y. Fox, and Dean L. May. *Building the City of God.* Salt Lake City: Deseret Book, 1976.

Beecher, Maureen Ursenbach. "Leonora, Eliza, and Lorenzo." *Ensign,* June 1980, pp. 64–69.

Romney, Thomas C. *The Life of Lorenzo Snow.* Salt Lake City: Sugarhouse Press, 1955.

Smith, Eliza R. Snow, *Biography and Family Record of Lorenzo Snow.* Salt Lake City: Deseret News Company, 1884.

Joseph F. Smith

Arrington, Leonard J. *From Quaker to Latter-day Saint: Bishop Edwin D. Woolley.* Salt Lake City: Deseret Book, 1976.

Bosworth, Norman S. "Remembering Joseph F. Smith, Loving Father, Devoted Prophet." *Ensign,* June 1983, pp. 21–24.

Corbett, Don Cecil. *Mary Fielding Smith: Daughter of Britain.* Salt Lake City: Deseret Book, 1966.

Gibbons, Francis M. *Joseph F. Smith: Patriarch and Preacher, Prophet of God.* Salt Lake City: Deseret Book, 1984.

Smith, Joseph Fielding. *Life of Joseph F. Smith.* Salt Lake City: Deseret News Press, 1938.

Heber J. Grant

Casper, Bernice Grant (grandniece of Heber J. Grant), personal interview with. Midvale, Utah, December 1988.

Hinckley, Bryant S. *Heber J. Grant: Highlights in the Life of a Great Leader.* Salt Lake City: Deseret Book, 1951.

Jacobsen, Florence Smith (granddaughter of Heber J. Grant), personal interview with. Salt Lake City, December 1988.

Walker, Ronald W. "Young Heber J. Grant's Years of Passage." *BYU Studies,* 24 (Spring 1984): 131–149.

George Albert Smith

Austin, Nancy Elliot (granddaughter of George Albert Smith), personal interview with. San Jose, California, November 1988.

Hatch, Martha Stewart (granddaughter of George Albert Smith), personal interview with. Socorro, New Mexico, November, 1988.

Improvement Era, April 1950. Special issue dedicated to President George Albert Smith. Articles: "A Day with the President," "A Normal Day," "After Eighty Years," "An Exemplar to All Men," "Born of Goodly Parents," "When the Grass Grew," "Service and Industry," "Humor— A Way of Life," and "Sharing the Gospel with Others."

Larsen, Shauna Stewart (granddaughter of George Albert Smith), personal interview with. Champagne, Illinois, November 1988.

"Papers of the George A. Smith Family." Special Collections, University of Utah, Salt Lake City, Utah.

Pusey, Merlo. *Builders of the Kingdom: George A. Smith, John Henry Smith, George Albert Smith.* Provo, Utah: Brigham Young University Press, 1981.

Smith, W. Whitney (nephew of George Albert Smith), personal interview with. Logan, Utah, July, 1988.

Stubbs, Glen R., "A Biography of George Albert Smith, 1870 to 1951" doctoral dissertation, presented to Brigham Young University, 1974.

David O. McKay

Gibbons, Francis M. *David O. McKay: Apostle to the World, Prophet of God.* Salt Lake City: Deseret Book, 1986.

McKay, David L. "Remembering Father and Mother, President David O. McKay and Sister Emma Ray Riggs McKay." *Ensign*, August 1984, pp. 34–40.

Middlemiss, Clare, comp. *Cherished Experiences from the Writings of President David O. McKay.* Salt Lake City: Deseret Book, 1955.

Morrell, Jeanette McKay. *Highlights in the Life of President David O. McKay.* Salt Lake City: Deseret Book, 1956.

Joseph Fielding Smith

Heslop, J. M., and Dell R. Van Orden. *Joseph Fielding Smith: A Prophet among the People.* Salt Lake City: Deseret Book, 1971.

Smith, Joseph Fielding, Jr., and John J. Stewart. *The Life of Joseph Fielding Smith.* Salt Lake City: Deseret Book, 1972.

Harold B. Lee

Clifton Ward Sunday School Minutes. Newell Hart Collection. USU Special Collections, Logan, Utah.

Goates, L. Brent. *Harold B. Lee: Prophet and Seer.* Salt Lake City: Bookcraft, 1985.

Henderson, Verena Howell. "History of Clifton, Idaho." Manuscript in Newell Hart Collection. USU Special Collections, Logan, Utah.

"In Memoriam." *Ensign*, February 1974, pp. 8–29, 75–96. Special section of articles on President Harold B. Lee. Articles: "The Long Odyssey," "Diary of Action: The Life and Administration of Harold B. Lee," "Speaking for Himself: President Lee's Stories," "Messages of Appreciation and Sympathy," "The Empty Room," "He Touched My Life," "A Sure Trumpet Sound: Quotations from President Lee," "Louisa Bingham Lee: Sacrifice and Spirit," "A Giant of a Man," "Harold Bingham Lee: Humility, Benevolence, Loyalty," "A True Servant of God," "In the Shadow of the Almighty."

1900 United States Census, Oneida County, Idaho. USU Special Collections, Logan, Utah.

Spencer W. Kimball

Kimball, Edward L., and Andrew E. Kimball, Jr. *Spencer W. Kimball.* Salt Lake City: Bookcraft, 1977.

———. *The Story of Spencer W. Kimball: A Short Man, a Long Stride.* Salt Lake City: Bookcraft, 1985.

Miner, Caroline E., and Edward L. Kimball. *Camilla.* Salt Lake City: Deseret Book, 1980.

Ezra Taft Benson

Arrington, Leonard J. "Idaho's Benson Family." *Idaho Heritage* 9 (1977): 9.

Benson, Ezra Taft. "Scouting Builds Men." *New Era*, February 1975, pp. 14–18.

Descendants of the George T. Benson, Jr., Family. Typescript, privately distributed, 1968.

Dew, Sheri. *Ezra Taft Benson: A Biography.* Salt Lake City: Deseret Book, 1987.

Leavitt, Melvin. "A Boy from Whitney." *New Era*, November 1986, pp. 20–31.

"Oral History, Ezra Taft Benson." *Idaho Heritage* 9 (1977): 15.

Petersen, Mark E. "President Ezra Taft Benson." *Ensign*, January 1986, pp. 2–13.

Peterson, Zetta Benson (cousin of Ezra Taft Benson), oral interview with. Logan, Utah, March 1986.

Whittle, Lera Benson (sister of Ezra Taft Benson), oral interview with. Provo, Utah, March 22, 1986.

Winward, Fielding (member of Ezra Taft Benson's Scout troop and Boy Scout chorus), oral interview with. Whitney, Idaho, February 28, 1989.

Howard W. Hunter

Faust, James E. "The Way of An Eagle." *Ensign*, August 1994, pp. 2–13.

"Howard W. Hunter: A Style of His Own." *New Era*, August 1994, pp. 4–7.

Huntsman, Jon M. "A Remarkable and Selfless Life." *Ensign*, April 1995, pp. 24–25.

Knowles, Eleanor. *Howard W. Hunter.* Salt Lake City: Deseret Book, 1994.

Meredith, Joleen. "Friend to Friend." *Friend*, October 1982, p. 6.

"President Howard W. Hunter, the Lord's 'Good and Faithful Servant.'" *Ensign*, April 1995, pp. 8–17.

Ricks, Kellene. "Friend to Friend." *Friend*, April 1990, p. 6.

Todd, Jay M. "President Howard W. Hunter: Fourteenth President of the Church." *Ensign*, July 1994, pp. 2–7.

Gordon B. Hinckley

Hinckley, Bryant Stringham. "The Autobiography of Bryant Stringham Hinckley." Compiled by Ruth Hinckley Willes. Church Historical Library.

Hinckley, Gordon B. "Gordon Bitner Hinckley." Appendix in "The Autobiography of Bryant Stringham Hinckley," compiled by Ruth Hinckley Willes. Church Historical Library.

———. "Some Lessons I Learned as a Boy." *Ensign*, May 1993, pp. 52–59.

———. "We Have a Work to Do." *Ensign*, May 1995, pp. 87–88.

"Gordon B. Hinckley: Man of Integrity, Fifteenth President of the Church." 59 minutes. The Church of Jesus Christ of Latter-day Saints, 1995. Videocassette.

Holland, Jeffrey R. "President Gordon B. Hinckley: Stalwart and Brave He Stands." *Ensign*, June 1995, pp. 2–13.

Peterson, Janet. "Friend to Friend." *Friend*, February 1987, pp. 6–7.

Todd, Jay M. "President Gordon B. Hinckley: Fifteenth President of the Church." *Ensign*, April 1995, pp. 2–7.

Index

Abbreviations for Church presidents are JS=Joseph Smith, Jr.; BY=Brigham Young; JT=John Taylor; WW=Wilford Woodruff; LS=Lorenzo Snow; JF=Joseph F. Smith; HG=Heber J. Grant; GS=George Albert Smith; DM=David O. McKay; JFielding=Joseph Fielding Smith; HL=Harold B. Lee; SK=Spencer W. Kimball; EB=Ezra Taft Benson; HH=Howard W. Hunter; GH=Gordon B. Hinckley